No Regrets?

Facing up to my Dad's Rejection

Colin Walters

Names, dates and places have been changed to protect the innocent (and not so innocent)

"You can't go back and change the beginning, but you can start where you are and change the ending"

C.S. Lewis

I sat waiting as patiently as I could. I could see people through the window of the door painstakingly rifling through files and looking up things on microfiche, maybe finding out their own family histories. I wondered what news I'd get. I took a deep breath and tried to look relaxed, although I doubt anyone could see me, so there was really no reason in keeping up appearances. The lobby of the Essex Records Office was pleasant enough, although unmistakably a local council building. A feint musk hung in the air giving the feel of a library or a school, which in a weird way was both comforting and unnerving at the same time. I'd always wondered what the inside of this building looked like, and now that I knew, it was admittedly a bit of an anti-climax. The building was just outside Chelmsford city centre, on the river, and I had walked past it several times. It was such a modern looking building from the outside. I remember it being built around 15 years ago and at the time I thought it was going to be a cinema or a leisure centre; it was a striking white building with a white metal roof that curved upwards like the end of a skateboard and I was a little disappointed when I found out it was going to be the new records office for Essex. Aside from the glass and steel staircase that took me up to the first-floor lobby, it was pretty generic inside. The walls were whitewashed, and the floor was laid with navy carpet tiles. The receptionist was sat behind a glass window with a wooden frame and a small opening with a metal tray beneath it, like in a bank. There was a wooden security door with a glass pane to the left that she would buzz people in to access files if they had a valid pass. I didn't have a pass.

What news would I get? Would I finally find out anything about my dad? I hadn't seen or heard from him in about 35 years. He had decided he wanted to cut ties with me and my sister when we were 8 or 9 after a pretty acrimonious divorce from my mum. He told us to our faces in front of my mum and a welfare officer in a local government building in a very firm but calm and unemotional way that he wasn't going to see us anymore. It was something that has stayed with me ever since and undoubtedly had a significant impact on me. But I've always wanted to know what happened next. Did he go off and have a wonderful life? Was he dogged with regret and remorse? I was hoping for a combination of the two to be completely honest. A few years ago, in 2015, I'd researched my family tree to see if I could find out whether he was still alive and whether I'd be able to find him, using *ancestry.co.uk*. I didn't want to make contact – but just to know whether he was alive or dead would have been enough at the time. My search didn't bring up anything other than finding out that my grandmother, his mum, had died in 1994, around the same time that my mum's mum had died; other confirmations of dates of birth and death that I already knew; and also, some historic information about my great grandparents and other ancestors that my mum didn't even know. But nothing about my dad. I put it out of my head until now and I'm not really sure why it suddenly came back with a vengeance. I'd flown back from a holiday in the Cyclades the night before with a group of three friends. It had been an amazing holiday. We'd started off staying for a few days in a beautiful hotel in Santorini, then taken the ferry to Paros and stayed in a villa halfway up a mountain. It had an incredible view and overlooked the town and the port, and you could see the Aegean Sea stretching out into the distance. Paros doesn't have an airport so the only way of getting there was on a ferry and this meant that it was a much quieter island to relax in. It was bliss. The third leg of our trip was to Mykonos for a few days exploring the labyrinthian streets and enjoying the local bars and eateries. Our last full day was spent on Elia Beach and while I was sunbathing, soaking up the sights of the golden sands, the beautiful sapphire sea and the rugged scenery, and actually properly relaxing for the first time in a while, my dad popped into my head and the wondering started again – so much so that I couldn't stop thinking about him for the rest of the trip and all the way home. So, I decided to find out what I could once and for all.

I think that back in 2015 and again now, I just wanted closure. I wasn't expecting to be able to meet up for a beer with him, arms outstretched in paternal love, sweeping the last 35 years or so to one side as if they never happened. The thought of that actually filled me with terror. I had wondered whether he'd ever wanted to find us again; whether he'd realised he'd made a terrible mistake and wanted to make amends. But he could have found us if he'd wanted; I moved out when I was 21 and my mum and my sister, Olivia, lived in the same house for a few years after that so he had a good 12 to 13 years to change his mind. And even now, he could have found us on social media relatively easily if he'd wanted. Having said that, I'd searched for him on Facebook, Twitter and Instagram amongst others, but nothing came up that matched his name and personal details.

I guess I also wanted to know why. How can you explain abandoning your children when they are still *children*, caught up in the middle of a divorce that had nothing to do with them and they didn't understand? It's only now when I look back as an adult, seeing friends with their children, seeing Olivia with her daughter, my niece, Louise of 8 years old, that I fail to understand his decision even more than I did when I was a child. Maybe I hadn't started my search earlier because I was scared of being rejected for a second time; it hurt bad enough the first time and maybe it was easier to not know what was on his mind despite the longing to find out. It was incredible the power he still held over me considering the length of time he'd been gone. There was a part of me that also worried about what my mum would think if I did find him. Would she think I was betraying her or being disloyal? I was probably closer to my mum now than I ever had been, but we'd had times when we clashed terribly, and growing up, she'd made some ridiculous decisions that made things so much more difficult than they needed to be. But she stuck around when my dad had left us in the lurch. And she struggled to raise us in impossible circumstances; looking back I've no idea how she did and how any of us survived. And she provided for us. And she loved us.

It was a beautiful sunny day and having spent the first night in a couple of weeks, back in my own bed, I'd slept better than I expected to. I had woken up around 9am and had made an effort to dress nicely. I wanted to make a nice impression for some reason. If I was to ask about my absent father who'd abandoned me as a child, I wanted whomever I was talking to, to understand that I had made something of my life and I wasn't a down and out. I was successful and polite and well dressed. So, I wore some smart jeans and picked out a smartly casual shirt. I'd looked on the Essex Records Office website last night to see whether I needed to do any preparation and the instructions simply stated there was no need – bring what information you have, and the team of professional staff would be able to provide expert advice. I downloaded the *Ancestry* app on my phone again and made sure I was able to log in and access the information I'd collated in 2015. All set.

The receptionist, a girl in her mid-twenties, although wearing a brown cardigan which made her look older than her years, had initially been a bit frosty. I had hesitantly asked to find out some information about someone. (I couldn't bring myself to explain that the 'someone' was my dad. I had felt a little embarrassed.) What information? Well, whether they were alive or dead would have been a start, I'd said, and the rather abrupt instruction coming back was initially to order a death certificate. The fee would be payable and non-refundable even if there was no death certificate on record. She had raised her eyebrows matter-of-factly as she explained the procedure. Although a bit taken aback, at £13 including postage I thought I'd take a punt and started filling in the form with everything I could remember (for the life of me I couldn't remember my dad's full date of birth – I knew he was born in March 1944 but the *Ancestry* app showed April – the receptionist explained that was probably when the birth was recorded). I had to state my relationship to the 'subject' on the form and when the receptionist saw that he was my dad she visibly softened and looked at me sympathetically – I guess this was also what I was initially trying to avoid – pity from strangers – but she then offered to see what she could find before I committed my £13. And so there I was, having taken a seat in the lobby, waiting patiently. My heart was beating ever so slightly faster than usual. I took another deep breath.

It had been about 10 minutes or so before the receptionist came into the lobby. She was smiling awkwardly. Actually, was it a grimace? I'm not convinced she was sure herself.

"I think I've found a match."

"A match?" My heart stopped for a second. But then, "What have you found a match for?"

"I *think* I've found a death certificate."

I paused as the news hit me. "How sure are you?" My heart was pounding now, and my mouth went dry. I swallowed a couple of times.

"I'm err… I'm *pretty* sure." She shifted uncomfortably.

I swallowed a couple of times more, trying to process the information. "Can you show it to me?"

"No, I'm… I'm sorry."

"Can you give me any information on it?"

"No – it's not an authorised copy so I can't give you any information. But you can order it and it'll be with you within 5 working days." The awkward, sympathetic smile reappeared.

"OK… Sure, that's fine."

I walked back to the window as the receptionist retreated through the door and gingerly sat back down behind her desk. I gave over my credit card details and then that was it: I had ordered a death certificate to check whether my father had in fact died. The ridiculousness of the situation swept over me and I felt ashamed at having to be told by a stranger that my father had died, maybe years ago. I then felt sorry for the receptionist who looked increasingly uncomfortable, as though she wasn't used to dealing with situations like this. I just needed to leave as soon as possible. My legs were slightly shaking as I walked down the glass and steel staircase, out the door and back to my car in Baddow Road car park. It felt like a much longer walk than it was on the way in and I resisted the urge to run, paranoid that someone might see me. I got to my car and sat in the carpark for a good 15 minutes trying to take it in. My dad had died. My dad had actually died. *Or had he?* I'd have to wait for the death certificate to really know for sure. I kept going over how the receptionist broke the news. How sure was she? She was 'pretty sure'. Those were the words she used, weren't they? How sure is 'pretty sure'? It's not 100%-without-a-doubt sure. But 'pretty sure' probably means sure enough otherwise she wouldn't have said it. Would she?

When I got home, I felt restless and didn't know what to do with myself. My head was racing with thoughts of my dad and old memories of happier times with him. The time when we built a plywood aeroplane together in the garden one summer; at Christmas opening presents in the living room and him faithfully telling us that Father Christmas had indeed eaten the mince pie and drunk the sherry we'd left for him; when he made me and Olivia laugh so much she wet herself while she was on his shoulders and that made us all laugh even more. And the family holidays to the Isle of Wight and the first time we all went on a plane to Torremolinos. But then the thoughts turned to what happened later. The blazing rows he and my mum had. The day he left. The times when we waited for him to take us out for the day and we'd had our coat and shoes on, and he never showed up. The day he told us he wasn't going to see us again and the way he looked at us – he looked *through* us rather than *at* us and didn't waver a bit. And that was the last I saw him.

How did I feel? I don't know. I guess I was shocked in a way; shocked that I'd got closer to finally finding out what happened to my dad after all these years of wondering what the hell happened. I secretly wanted the death certificate to be his and then immediately felt bad for feeling that way. I just didn't want to have got this far and then find out that it was all a false alarm. I remember when I was younger, thinking that it would have been easier if he had died. At least then I'd have believed that he still loved us.

I started to unpack my suitcase from my holiday to use up some of my pent-up energy and focus my mind, and put the first load of laundry on. That seemed to help me calm down a little and when I felt OK, I decided to call my mum.

"Hi Mum, it's me."

"Hi dear, how are you? Did you have a nice holiday? The pictures you took looked wonderful!"

"Yes, it was great thanks. I really managed to relax. How have you been?"

"Oh, I'm ok thanks. My arthritis in my neck has been giving me grief and I've used up so much *Deep Heat* on it, but other than that I'm ok. Anita, my neighbour, you know – the 96-year old? She had a fall. She's fine other than a terrible bruise on her arm. I've told her so many times not to wear those blimmin' slippers indoors – I told her they'd be the death of her but she's a stubborn old thing. But I've been doing her shopping for her and I haven't had any time for myself!" I smiled at this last remark. My mum was retired and although she had a good social life, she had plenty of time on her hands and a few shopping trips wouldn't take up much of that. "Anyway, tell me about your holiday!"

"Well, before all of that, I think I've found out something about Dad…"

There was a pause before the inevitable question: "What have you done?" She sounded worried, suspicious, even.

"Look, I haven't *done* anything."

I explained the morning I'd had and the fact that it was very likely that he'd died. She asked the same unanswered questions I had in my head – When? How? How sure I was that it was him? I explained again that we'd know for sure and presumably we'd find out more when I received the death certificate. I told her that I couldn't remember his date of birth.

"14th March 1944." Mum was always good with dates. As soon as she told me I knew it to be true immediately.

My mum sounded emotional and her voice cracked.

"Mum, what's wrong? Are you ok?"

"I suppose I always hoped for a happy ending." She wasn't sobbing but was clearly quite emotional.

"Mum, I guess it's not a *sad* ending... It's just... An ending."

"Yes, but I always thought he'd make it up to you." This surprised me more than anything. Things were so bitter between the two of them I didn't expect her to feel any kind of sadness for the fact that he might have died. I had no idea she had wanted some kind of reconciliation for us. "I remember it hit you so hard when he left you. You more so than your sister, and I always hoped for your sake he'd come back at some point. And anyway, at the end of the day, he was your dad. And without him, I wouldn't have had you both."

"Oh, Mum, honestly, there's nothing we can do about it now is there?" I tried to comfort her in the best way that I could with empty reassurances, but I was a little taken aback and felt more emotional after hearing Mum's take on it.

"Are you going to tell Olivia?"

Olivia was older than me, but only by 15 months. She was at times incredibly emotional and there were certain things my mum and I had held back from telling her over the years to prevent a mini breakdown, and any difficult news that we did end up telling her, we'd devise a strategy to break it constructively, calmly and manage it in the best way so she wouldn't collapse in a heap.

"Look, if he has died, she has a right to know. I can't keep it from her, but I'd rather wait until I get the death certificate just to be sure. I don't want to tell her and then find out that it's not him. We're due to be going over to see her next weekend, aren't we? By then I should have received the death certificate and anyway I think face to face would be the best way."

So that was the initial plan.

Feeling a little better, I sat in my living room and again thought about my dad. I wondered if he'd have been proud of me. Things had not been easy since he left us, and life generally had been tough. As I grew older, I'd never really felt like I'd fitted in. Maybe that coincided with Dad leaving us; maybe it was a combination of several things. I'd had struggles at school, being picked on, which ultimately impacted my confidence and self-esteem. But I had always worked hard so that I could get good exam results and get a good job. Financially things had been incredibly difficult at home, so I had been determined not to find myself in the same position as an adult. I was a creative child, always interested in art and drawing, but the career advice I'd received was that a good job was in the financial sector, in an office, so that's what I aimed for. After my A-Levels, I had got a job at a local insurance company, which I admittedly quite enjoyed. I liked working towards targets and loved how I got recognition for the effort I put in. I made some really good friends, some of which I'm still in contact with now and my social life began to take off. After my mum's string of failed relationships and some heated rows at home, I had saved up and bought my first flat in Chelmsford aged 21 and with the equity that I gained during the late nineties and early noughties I was able to move into a lovely semi-detached Victorian house. By that time, I had worked my way up the corporate ladder within a multinational insurance company and was the European Operations Manager, responsible for the operations and underwriting support for 6 countries and travelled frequently to the continent. I had the odd trip to Miami too. After 4 years in that role, I had decided that I'd achieved all I could and needed to move on, so I ended up putting a paper together recommending my role was removed from the structure — which took me by surprise when it actually happened, and I was free to take redundancy. Despite the early mornings, late nights and intense deadlines I always got a little thrill boarding a plane or the Eurostar and I loved seeing the overseas teams and helping them with strategic solutions to some of the issues they were facing, so leaving was bittersweet but ultimately, I needed a new challenge and change of scenery. My redundancy pay was also generous – 4 weeks for every year I'd worked at the company and I'd been there over 14 years, so I paid a large chunk off my mortgage and took the summer off and it was bliss.

After a short stint at a different insurance company and realising the value of freelance contract work, I set up my own limited company and got a contract as a project manager. By this time, I'd moved house again into the Chelmsford district of Beaulieu in a new-build 3 storey townhouse. I never thought I'd ever be able to afford something like this and sometimes when I think back to how difficult things were financially as a child, I'm still a little overwhelmed that I managed to move here. This was my forever home and I loved it.

I had got through, but not completely unscathed. I suffered from crippling depression in the early 2010s and was on anti-depressants for a good few years. I remember the side effects that I suffered going on and coming off the pills almost being as bad as the depression itself, but ultimately, I learned a huge amount from that time. I grew a great deal as a person – I learned not to take things so personally and gained a lot of insight about my own mental state, my triggers and sometimes how to overcome them. But it's not something I would ever want to repeat or wish on anyone else. I also suffered from anxiety and was often plagued with self-doubt. It hit a high during the depression years but, I guess due to low self-esteem, I felt anxious in any new situation. Despite that, bizarrely I still pushed for redundancy a year or so later. But overall, I felt incredibly grateful for the life I'd created. I had a varied and lively social life with a wide circle of friends and was generally happy and content for the most part. The only thing missing was that I'd never had a long-term relationship (or many short-term relationships for that matter either). I had got very used to being on my own and hated the way online apps had replaced the more human side of dating. I was all too aware that I put barriers in front of anyone who came too close. No prizes for guessing where those issues arose from.

My phone buzzed to let me know a message had been received. It was Jane. Jane was a great friend and we'd grown closer over the past few years, maybe because of the tragedy that she had endured in her life. Following a seemingly blissful marriage and two children, her husband had told her he wanted a divorce, which was obviously devastating, but Jane was able to maintain composure and against all odds remained on good terms with her ex-husband. She'd found love again, relatively quickly with a lovely man called Peter, who worshipped her, and had remarried a few years after the divorce. However, when they were away celebrating their first wedding anniversary, Peter suffered a fatal heart attack whilst they were having a romantic dinner together in a restaurant. He was only 39 years old. It goes without saying she was devastated and sought grief counselling to get through the unbearable pain. She suddenly found herself divorced and widowed before the age of 40. But she remained incredibly strong, as she was with her divorce. She recalls that last day they'd spent together as one of the happiest times of her life and remained philosophical, not once complaining, becoming bitter or seeing herself as a victim. I've always admired Jane for her matter-of-factness, her almost stubborn like strength, and her no-nonsense approach. She had a vulnerability about her, which made her human and approachable and lovely, but you knew exactly where you stood with her. Maybe tragedy attracts tragedy? I saw Jane as a kindred spirit, especially during the last few years.

I read her message – a reminder of a planned coffee and catch up tomorrow which I'd completely forgotten about. My heart soared as I responded quickly, suggesting we go to Coffee Squared, an independent coffee shop a short walk from where I lived. She came back, planning to drive to mine for about 11.30. It would be so good to see Jane! It would be great to get her perspective on the news I'd received and interesting to see what advice she'd give me.

I could imagine that behind Jane's sunglasses her eyes had widened. Her long, streaked hair fell loosely around her shoulders, framing her pretty face. She was dressed casually in jeans and a dark blue tee shirt with white printed flowers.

"How are you feeling now? You seem... *ok*?" She was hesitant in her assessment as I sensed her eyeing me carefully, looking ready for any potential emotional breakdowns.

I glanced around. We were sitting outside Coffee Squared on a small patio area where there were around 9 tables, making the most of the late summer weather. Coffee Squared had been open for about a year and had quickly garnered a loyal following with the local community, despite a Costa Coffee shop only a few minutes away. It was friendly and quirky and offered something maybe a little more authentic than the mainstream alternative. The patio overlooked some landscaped gardens and a small, paved carpark, which was virtually empty as most customers had walked here. The sky was a beautiful azure blue, and the sun was streaming down. But I was also relieved I had an excuse to hide behind my sunglasses. There was a nice gentle hum of conversation and crockery clinking in the background and we were lucky to have found a free table. Jane had just arrived back from the counter with a latte for me and a cappuccino for her, both in oversized mugs with a small biscotti biscuit. I sat back in my chair and held my latte thoughtfully. I'd had a restless night and had been fully awake since about 5.30 this morning, watching and waiting for the morning sun eventually to rise and peek through the blinds. Although I was still tired, I couldn't get comfortable enough to fully relax, which was ironic because the night before, the first time I'd slept in my own bed for two weeks, the familiar feel of the mattress and pillows were such a welcome change from the places I'd stayed. The news was beginning to sink in a bit more but was still whirling around in my head. I had so many questions and I just wanted to know for sure whether the death certificate related to my dad or not. I had an uneasy feeling in my stomach, but I didn't really feel particularly emotional; I was more reflective than anything else.

"I'm ok, I think. I just want to know for sure now."

"Do you mind me asking what exactly happened? You've never really spoken about your dad before... I only know that you hadn't seen him since you were young."

I took a deep breath as I began to recall everything that happened all those years ago. Although it had been going around my head the night before, it honestly felt like a different lifetime, it was so remote and removed from the life I lived now, and I hadn't spoken about it for so long. I took a large sip from my latte before I began my story.

"My mum and dad split when I was young – I think I was about 7 years old and initially, believe it or not, it felt like a good thing to have happened, after the initial shock. My mum had been unhappy for a while and I know she'd had an affair, which I think my dad knew about... I'm not entirely sure about that. Although he'd moved out of the family home in Elm Park – he moved back in with his mum in Hackney – Dad would often come round for dinner and it was very amicable between my mum and dad; he was still about regularly but without any of the arguments. I don't think we ever missed him at that time. He worked shifts as an HGV driver, delivering beer to breweries, so it wouldn't be unusual for him not be home when we got back from school, or in the mornings when we woke up and sometimes when we went to bed. And he would also take us out for the day, so we probably saw him more than we would normally have done. I know he wanted to get back with my mum, but she just wasn't interested. My dad was always a very kind, easy going man… and I guess maybe a little soft. He was happy enough to go along with anything my mum suggested, and I think she wanted someone to take control more… She didn't want to be wearing the trousers or make all the decisions. Anyway, things changed when my mum started seeing someone new – a man called Alf – and me and my sister both really didn't like him. He had a violent temper and would blow up quite unpredictably, completely different to my dad. But when my dad found out about Alf, I think that must have given him the kick to find someone new and move on himself. He started seeing a lady called Siobhan who was quite a bit younger than him – I think up to about ten years younger.

"Now, Siobhan didn't like me or my sister and when she started to come along on days out with us, there would be the odd dig… There was one time, I remember we were in the back of my dad's car and Siobhan was in the front and she looked back at us with a sneer on her face and said to my dad something like: 'I don't like the kids' names at all. Was it Margaret [my mum] who chose them?' I remember she said it with such distain in her voice and even then, as a child I almost rolled my eyes and thought what a stupid, childish thing to say. My dad said 'Yes, yes it was Margaret who chose the kids' names.' Me and my sister both knew that was rubbish because my sister was named after Olivia Newton-John, who was my dad's favourite actress. But he just agreed with her."

I shook my head in incredulation and Jane mirrored the movement. "That's a ridiculous thing to say!"

"Yes, I know. There were other things – little things, subtle enough to get through without my dad really acknowledging them, but significant for us both to notice. And then as time went on, there were times he'd arrange to take us out and he'd not show up – that became more and more frequent. After that, arguments about maintenance money all began to kick off. I remember a furious row on the doorstep of the Elm Park house with my mum, dad and Siobhan, in front of the whole street, EastEnders style! The fact that Alf was now in the picture, my dad, no doubt because of Siobhan, said he shouldn't have to pay maintenance for us. It was ridiculous because my mum's relationship with Alf was on the rocks and after we initially moved in with him quite quickly, we'd just as quickly moved out into a small house in South Woodham Ferrers. But even so, things started getting nasty – he and Siobhan would follow my mum around to prove that she was working; we were also followed briefly and there would be photos taken of us, I think to show we were well dressed and better off than my mum claimed, when in reality we were wearing second-hand clothes from charity shops and we were on benefits. He even went as far as getting my mum arrested."

"What? *Arrested?* What for?" Jane was leaning forward now; her mouth was slightly open, and her brow was furrowed. I took another gulp of latte as I formulated my thoughts.

"Back when we lived in Elm Park with my dad, there was a policeman called Paul who lived across the road, who my dad was quite friendly with. One morning in the South Woodham Ferrers house, we were getting ready for school and there was a knock at the door. Two plain clothed policemen placed my mum under arrest and took her away in an unmarked police car. I remember that my mum had been in the middle of ironing my sister's school skirt and pleaded with them to let her finish before she was taken away. You can imagine that me and my sister were absolutely hysterical. My sister was making so much noise, our next-door neighbour came out to see what was going on and thank goodness was able to follow my mum to the police station she was taken to. Another neighbour offered to look after us for the day. When my mum got to the police station, she was told she was being arrested for store card fraud, because of camping equipment that had been bought without permission in a branch of Debenhams. Now my mum is the most unlikely person to want to go camping you'd ever meet! But the police can apparently hold someone for up to 24 hours on suspicion of any crime with no evidence. My mum saw Paul and when she asked him what was going on, he said simply: 'You've heard of a woman scorned – this is what happens when a man is scorned.'

"My mum was held for most of the day in a prison cell and was released quite late that night. We spent the day worried and tearful and to think my dad must have known the impact it would have had on us, knowing there was no-one guaranteed to look after us, and still wanted it to happen to teach my mum some kind of lesson. I remember feeling exhausted when she came back through the door and feeling so relieved that she was ok. We'd waited up for her to come back, not really knowing whether she would. She looked awful though – she was so pale, and her eyes were swollen from crying. I remember she held us tight for ages.

"Anyway, after that, things came to a head and we ended up going to a mediation meeting with a welfare officer – looking back I've no idea why me and my sister we there; surely it should just have been between my mum and my dad – but ultimately we had to recount the times we'd seen my dad and where we were taken and sometimes with the questioning and the persistence of the welfare officer, coupled with the circumstances it became a little difficult and emotional. I remember there was a moment when I was getting a bit tearful and the welfare officer said to my dad:

'Your son's crying. Are you going to comfort him?' and without even looking at me, my dad said: 'He always cries.'

"At the end of the meeting, just before he left, he sat me and my sister down and said to us as clear as anything: 'Look, I know you're both being well looked after so I think it's best if I don't see you anymore.' And that was it. He left and that was the last any of us ever saw him. The last thing that happened was that there was a court hearing, and my mum was properly stitched up. My mum's solicitor for some reason didn't think it was worth attending the hearing I think because an agreement had been reached and was told it just needed to be rubber stamped, so my mum was on her own and they basically said that all ties were going to be cut and maintenance would no longer be provided, and my mum was left with very little. Things were clearly hugely different back then!"

"What about his family? Did you have any uncles or aunts from your dad's side? What about your grandparents?"

"We lost contact with everyone. My granddad on my dad's side had died a few years before when my parents were still together, but my nan was still alive and I had an Uncle Harry and an Aunty Deb, and cousins who we've never seen since all this happened."

I paused as Jane took this in. We sat in silence for a couple of minutes. She looked thoughtful but had a furrowed brow as she considered the story I'd just told her.

"How do you feel about your dad now? Are you angry with him? The whole thing sounds awful and I wouldn't blame you if you held some resentment towards him."

I took a large sip of latte again as I thought this through. "I'm not angry or bitter anymore, but there was a time when I was; I remember the hardest times when we had no money and as kids we didn't have new clothes or the latest toys or stuff like that – and my mum really struggled to put food on the table… And I never had a male role model to help me through the difficult teenage years, so there were times when I blamed him for everything that was wrong in the world and hated him. But as I grew older, those feelings began to fade, and I came to accept the situation more and, I guess control my own destiny. He had always been so kind and gentle up to that point, but he changed so much with Siobhan, I often blamed her more than him. But ultimately it was his decision to do what he did.

"It was when my niece was born when it hit me most. The ridiculous overwhelming love I felt for this person as she came into the world – and she wasn't even mine! To think we were a similar age to what Louise is now and I can't imagine even thinking about not seeing her again. He really sacrificed a lot for Siobhan… It was him missing out on the most formative years of our lives – his children's lives. The more I've thought about it over the past few days I wondered whether he ever had any regrets."

"He must have had regrets." Jane was adamant. "I can't see any parent not having regrets about what he did!"

"I guess so. But he chose to keep to his word and not see us anymore."

"Do you think that he was scared of the reaction he'd get if he did come looking for you?"

"Maybe. Who's to know now? I do hope he was happy. What a waste if he wasn't."

"What were you looking for?" said Jane suddenly, "I mean, when you went into the Essex Records Office yesterday, did you want to find him? Alive, I mean? Would you have wanted to meet him?"

I took a deep breath as I considered this. "I don't know. I didn't think so yesterday. Actually, I wasn't sure I would find anything – and I'm not sure I was really prepared to find this out. Having slept on it, I guess it would have been nice to have made peace with him. Maybe I was scared of being rejected again, but after all this time I just want a bit more closure. But if it is him, it'll be interesting to see what's on his death certificate. I wonder what else I'll find out."

"Don't expect too much. If he died in hospital, there might not be that much more information… I'm trying to remember what was on Peter's death certificate. I haven't really looked at it in too much detail to be honest!" She took a pause before she considered her next question. "What are you going to do if it is him? I mean, will that be enough, or will you want more so that you can get closure?"

It was a good question and one I hadn't yet contemplated. "I don't know! I guess I won't really know until it arrives. I really hope it comes through soon."

"Have you… thought about counselling? It sounds like you've had a difficult time of it when you were young and if you're looking for answers now, it might be the right time to get some professional help."

I knew Jane was right. But I didn't feel quite ready for counselling yet. I'm not sure I was in the right frame of mind and probably wasn't ready to open up Pandora's box and deal with everything that would inevitably spill out.

Jane asked about my mum's reaction and I explained the conversation I'd had yesterday and the plan we had made to tell my sister depending on what would land on my door mat within the next few days. Jane nodded in approval.

"Look, I'm always here if you need to talk it through. You do seem remarkably calm and I don't think it's properly hit you yet so if or when it does, please call."

"Thanks Jane – I really do appreciate it."

I suppose I was calm. Jane was right as usual, that the news hadn't properly sunk in, but then it wasn't definite news yet. In some way I expected him to have died, although I would have thought it would show up on the search in 2015 through *Ancestry* if that had been the case. I still had my doubts.

Jane had to leave at around three o'clock to pick up her children from school, but it was great to catch up with her and get her insight. It was also nice to find out her news and what she'd been up to over the past couple of weeks. Jane had started seeing someone called Nick. It was early days, but she seemed quite keen and it was amazing to see her happy with him. He lived in Tunbridge Wells, so quite a drive to Chelmsford, but he was fluent in Italian, having lived there for a number of years. They'd been on a couple of dates and everything seemed to be going in the right direction so I really hoped it would work out. Jane had said previously that she didn't want another husband – just yet, anyway – but some fun and adventure would be nice. Good for her.

I called Olivia later that afternoon to check-in and confirm plans to visit her next weekend. She sounded irritated when she picked up the call.

"Hey, are you OK?" I proceeded cautiously, navigating waters that I didn't want to become stormy.

"Yes, it's just Kirstie. She's been a complete pain again." Kirstie was Olivia's stepdaughter and their relationship had been rocky to say the least.

"Why? What's happened now?"

"Well, she's taken to ignoring me now – in my own house! I don't know who she thinks she is. And Daniel doesn't do anything about it, so I've had it out with her myself. I told her that if she's going to spend time here, she should at least show me some respect. She just sits there and looks at her phone. She doesn't talk, she doesn't interact; I just get one-word answers from her and I've had enough of it all."

Daniel was Olivia's husband. They'd been married for just over two years after being together for about twelve years. Daniel had three children from a previous marriage, all of which had been troublesome in one way or another. Will, the eldest at 24 had two children with two different girls and hadn't taken responsibility for their upbringing or any real parenting. He currently lived off benefits in a caravan. Scott was the youngest at 16 and suffered from ADHD. Daniel's ex-wife and the children's mum, who he and Kirstie lived with, had refused to acknowledge that he had any issues and that he was just a little excitable, but this had created issues at school and then developed into some mental health issues for Scott, creating anxiety and agoraphobia for which he was thankfully now receiving treatment. And then Kirstie, who at 21, was one of the most obnoxious girls I'd ever met. I'd only seen her a handful of times myself and had always tried to make conversation with her, but as Olivia had suggested, she would only give back the least she could get away with – the odd word or a nod of the head without even any eye contact. It didn't even seem like she was shy; she was just rude.

I often admired Olivia for taking on all that she had. I'm not sure many other people her age would have done the same thing; the kids had all been hard work and Daniel had done little to properly manage the situation with their mum or with Olivia. It was far from easy and so far away from the blissful life she craved. After the birth of her daughter, Louise, she'd struggled going back to work on reduced hours and to keep a fraction of her take home pay due to the childcare costs she had to pay, as well as really missing her daughter. So, she decided to completely change direction and trained to become a childminder so she could spend time with Louise, whilst looking after other children and get paid for it. She studied and qualified within 6 months and then set up her own practice. She built up her business through word of mouth and I often marvel at her determination and work ethic.

"So, what happened next?"

"Well, I told Danny that he had to talk to her and so he sat her down and he was really good; he does back me up when he sees that she's wrong. He told her that she had to respect me, especially when she comes round here, and she got all upset, but when she calmed down, she did admit that she was wrong, so hopefully things will change, but who knows? I just don't like her!"

"OK, well hopefully – if Danny's had a word, then things *might* change." I tried to sound as optimistic as possible, but this situation was hardly new. It seemed like a repeating cycle every few weeks and Olivia would always get upset about something.

"Yeah, *hopefully*. Anyway, how was your holiday? The pictures looked amazing! Did you have a good time?"

"Yes, it was wonderful, thanks. The weather was incredible, and we had such a laugh."

"Aww I can't wait to hear all about it! Are you still coming round on Saturday?"

"Yes – that's what I was calling for. What time shall we aim to get to you?"

"How about one-ish? I'll do some lunch for us all."

"Brilliant, thanks. I'll let Mum know."

I felt ever so slightly anxious discussing the plans for next weekend, wondering whether I'd have some additional news to share. I tried not to think about it too much and the rest of the conversation remained light and good humoured.

The weekend was spent on chores - food shopping and getting ready for work: Ironing my shirts and collecting my dry cleaning. In January, I'd secured a job as a project manager in the city, overseeing the integration of two insurance brokers. I was responsible for the Continental Europe, Middle East and South Africa regions. It admittedly sounded a lot more impressive than it actually was; the local teams were good and knew exactly what they needed to do, and my job was to keep track of all the planned activities and to ensure everything was joined up and documented properly. Before my holiday, I'd spent a week in Dubai and then a week in Johannesburg, each with the legal and finance representatives to finalise the planning of the legal entity alignment, which was a fairly chunky and complicated piece of work, and I managed to convince my boss to let me fly business class to Johannesburg. It was a twelve-hour flight and there were only red-eyes scheduled, which landed early morning. I'd never flown business before, so it was a real thrill to 'turn left', change into pyjamas after dinner and be able to convert my seat into a bed. I didn't sleep as much as I'd hoped – there was a fair amount of turbulence and the lights came up around 5am so that breakfast could be served – but it was a much more enjoyable flight than had I been in Economy. All in all, it had been a busy couple of weeks and when I was on my flight back, knowing that work was finished now and my holiday in Greece was in front of me, I felt a great sense of relief.

On Monday 16th September, despite the initial holiday blues when I stood on the platform of Chelmsford Station, waiting for the 07:49 to Liverpool Street, it was great to see my colleagues again and catch up with the latest goings on. I went to lunch with two ladies that I sat near – Temi and Nancy. Temi was originally from Nigeria and Nancy was of Chinese descent but grew up in Switzerland. One of the reasons I loved working in London was the diversity and the cultural richness that I would never have been exposed to had I just lived and worked in Chelmsford. I'd met so many people over the years who'd become great friends. During January I'd travelled to Sydney and stayed with someone I used to work with in a previous company, and the year before I'd been invited to a wedding in Poland of a former colleague, which was the craziest wedding I'd ever been to! There was always something going on and people to meet up with for lunch or drinks after work.

After a long day of meetings, I came home and as I opened the door, I saw a plain brown A5 envelope on the mat. It had my name and address handwritten neatly on the front. The post mark was Chelmsford.

Was this it? My heart pumping, I carried the envelope through my kitchen to the dining room and sat down. I slowly opened it and took out the death certificate with the accompanying compliments slip from the Essex Records Office inside. I quickly scanned the document and saw immediately that it was my dad's:

Name and surname – James Edward Walters
Date and place of birth – Fourteenth March 1944, Hackney

I took a deep breath. It was him; *my dad. My dad had actually died.* I continued reading, breathing heavily.

Date and place of death – Thirtieth April 2016, 37 Crescent Drive Canvey Island.

Only three and a half years ago. He'd have been 72. And the previous search I did through *Ancestry* was in 2015 so that's why he never showed up.

Cause of death I (a) Motor Neurone Disease.

Motor Neurone Disease? What an awful way to die. A wave of emotion washed over me, and I suddenly felt such compassion and sympathy for this man who I used to know, who I hadn't seen for 35 years, who happened to be our dad.

Name and surname of informant – Siobhan Patricia O'Reilly.

Siobhan? The same Siobhan he was with all those years ago? He must have been happy to have stayed with her all that time?

Qualification – Causing body to be cremated.

My heart sank at this latest fact. I had wondered if I'd be able to find out where he was buried so I could at least visit his grave, but I wasn't able to do that if he'd been cremated. 37 Crescent Drive in Canvey Island was also the address listed for Siobhan and shown as my dad's usual address. Canvey was only a 25-minute drive away. I shook my head at the irony of him being that close to us for all those years.

So many mixed emotions competed for my headspace; moments of sorrow and regret coupled with bittersweet feelings, remembering the happier times with him, and then again recalling the bad times leading up to him cutting all ties with us. I couldn't stop wondering whether he ever regretted what he did, even fleetingly during his last moments? Did he ever wonder what happened to his children? Was he tormented by the fact that we were virtual strangers? Would he have contacted us had he been able to? I got up from my chair and paced around the room, breathing deeply, trying to process everything. I walked over to the kitchen and poured myself a large glass of water and drank it down in a few greedy gulps. After about ten minutes I'd managed to calm myself down a bit and picked up my phone.

"Mum, it's him. I've got the death certificate and it's him."

"Definitely?"

"Yes – date and place of birth, full name – complete match." I expected my mum to sound frantic or even a little emotional. To the contrary, she sounded relatively calm, albeit slightly bewildered.

"What else does it say?"

"Mum, he died in April 2016 – only 3 and a half years ago – so that's why he didn't show up on the *Ancestry* search. But he died from Motor Neurone Disease.

"Oh God, really? That's a terrible illness! I hope he didn't suffer too much!"

"I think he was still with Siobhan. She's named on the death certificate. Was her surname O'Reilly?"

"I knew she had an Irish name – that must be her. Christ - he stayed with her all that time." My mum paused, and I could picture her shaking her head. "Well, I hope they were happy if they were together for all those years." She didn't sound vindictive. Her tone was thoughtful; philosophical even. "So, you're going to tell Olivia on Saturday then?"

"Yes. I can't keep it from her. She has a right to know. Like we said, I'll wait until she goes out to the kitchen to make us drinks, and then while she's on her own I'll nip out and tell her then. How do you think she'll react?"

"You know your sister. I think she'll be upset but hopefully there won't be too much drama. How are you feeling about it all?"

"I don't know. I guess a little shocked by the whole thing really; lots of information to take in, but at least now we know."

After I put the phone done to my mum, I googled Motor Neurone Disease and found out that most people only survived between 2 and 5 years after diagnosis. I thought of the brilliant physicist Stephen Hawking in his wheelchair, only able to speak through a computer; unable to properly move, his body twisted and contorted from the ravages of the disease, and I contrasted that with my dad, how I remembered him: Fit and strong and healthy, able to pick me up and swing me around. I could hear his laugh as I screamed out to go higher and his strong arms as he gently lifted me down. I remembered his voice reading me a bedtime story; how he tucked me in and the stubbly kiss on my cheek as he said goodnight. I couldn't imagine that strong, fit, healthy man reduced to the frail, weak, person that I no longer knew and would now never meet again.

The next few days were odd. My head was consumed with thoughts of my dad and how he died, wondering what kind of life he would have lived; wondering what could have been and how different my life would be had he played a part in it. I went round to see Jane on Thursday evening after work and talked it through with her. It was always good to go through the motions with Jane.

"What are you going to do now? Are you going to do anything else? You have Siobhan's address. You could contact her? I can see you still have lots of questions, so you could reach out to her and see what she says?" The thought had crossed my mind but the sneer on Siobhan's face appeared in my mind as I considered it.

"Siobhan hated us! She was probably the reason he didn't want to see us anymore."

"But that was 30 odd years ago. Look at how differently *you* think about it now – you don't have any bitterness, do you?" Jane eyed me carefully, not entirely convinced the question she asked was completely rhetorical.

"No, I don't. I genuinely don't."

"Well, then. Why should she still hold any resentment towards you? She got everything she wanted and spent the best years of her life with him. It's understandable for anyone to be curious about their relatives, especially one of their parents! If anything, she might be feeling a little guilty now, so she might want to make it up to you."

I reflected on this over the next few days. I did feel like I wanted more answers but wasn't sure about getting in contact with Siobhan, not yet anyway. I thought I'd deal with Olivia first before deciding to do anything.

<u>Saturday 21st September</u>

My mum lived in Chelmer Village, a ten-minute drive from where I lived, and I was able to see her at least once every couple of weeks. She lived in a ground floor maisonette at the end of a cul-de-sac, with a beautiful garden of flowers and shrubs that she'd lovingly curated over the past ten or so years she'd lived there. Olivia lived in Ipswich. She'd moved there to be with Daniel, who grew up there. I would drive up to see them with mum in tow every couple of months and she'd come down to see us, either at my mum's or round to me around the same frequency so we got to see each other about once a month.

It was midday when I arrived outside Mum's, and as I unclicked my seatbelt and got out of the car, I saw her appear at the door. It was a bright day, but a slight chill in the air indicated that autumn was on its way. I breathed in the fresh air, enjoying the coolness and waited for Mum before I got back in. As my mum walked over, I noticed how frail she had become. She was 77 now. She opened the door and groaned as she climbed inside.

"You OK?" I asked.

"Yes, I'm just getting old," she chuckled. "Right, I'm in."

My mum was a notoriously nervous passenger, so I always chose music carefully on our way to Ipswich to keep her in a calm mood. Sometimes it would be Barbra Streisand, Luther Vandross or even Jack Savoretti, whose music I'd recently introduced her to, and she loved. This time however, it was the turn of Diana Ross. I gently pulled away and headed towards the A12 as *Touch Me in The Morning* began to emanate from the speakers. I was careful not to go above 60 miles per hour, as always when I drove my mum to Ipswich.

"And how are you feeling about all of this?" she enquired, "You've had a couple of days for it to sink in."

"I'm ok, I think. I still feel quite reflective. I'm just shocked at the way he died." I'd done some more googling of Motor Neurone Disease and there was a hereditary link. Around 10% of people who were diagnosed had relatives who'd previously suffered from it. Trying to be positive I guess that meant that I (and Olivia) had a 90% chance of *not* getting it, but I'd made a conscious note to see my GP to understand whether there was anything we could do to delay or prevent it. Although it sounded awful and it was a slow degenerative disease for which there was no cure, it didn't appear to be particularly painful and medication was available which helped to reduce the symptoms and the impact it would have on a life.

Mum and I went over the plan again and I reiterated that when Olivia went out to the kitchen to make drinks, I'd follow her and break it to her gently. I had the death certificate with me to show her; I'd put it in the cup holder of my car so that my mum could see it. She picked it up and after taking her glasses out of her bag and putting them on, reviewed it carefully.

"Yep, it's definitely him. Funny that they ended up in Canvey?"

I nodded. Canvey Island was where Alf had lived and where we moved to after we left Elm Park, so there was history there. I didn't remember it that well as we only spent a matter of months there before my mum and Alf split up. I wonder how long they'd lived there – was it within the last few years so they could live by the coast?

"He did love you." My mum spoke carefully and deliberately as she said this. It took me by surprise, and I wasn't sure how to acknowledge it; I hesitated, remembering that he must have loved us, but within him something had snapped, and things must have changed. "He did. I know he did – both you and your sister. And you don't just stop loving your children. It's something that never changes, no matter how old you both get, so I bet he must have had some terrible regrets. Every birthday, every Christmas, every Easter, he must have thought of you both and wondered what you were doing, what you'd made of your lives, how your personalities had developed." She paused for a moment as she chose her words. "And he would have been fine with the fact you're gay. He wouldn't have had any issues with that, I'm sure of it."

This had been in the back of my mind ever since 2015 when I first started my initial search. I'd wondered what my dad's reaction would have been if he was still around and I had to tell him. Would he have been disappointed? Would he feel let down? I'd like to think not; again, thinking back to the soft and gentle man he was, I'd hope he'd have accepted me.

"Well, that doesn't matter now, does it? What's done is done and there are things we'll probably never find out." I tried to sound matter of fact and carefree, but I could feel the emotion rise up in me and I'm not sure I was able to hide it completely. We sat without saying anything else, enjoying the dulcet tones of Diana Ross and her greatest hits.

I remember my struggles with coming out all too vividly. I think I knew I was gay from about the age of 12 or so. I had the biggest crush on Matt Goss back in the day and convinced myself that it was a phase and that it would go away. Ironically the kids at school all had a better idea than I did, but the late eighties and early nineties were pretty hostile for closeted teens, and I was picked on mercilessly, called names and punched in the corridor. I ended up hating school as a teenager, but I doubt that anyone actually thought I was gay. The thought of coming out back then was unthinkable. It was when I was in my early twenties that I got to a point where I couldn't hide it any longer. I was 24, I think, and I decided to tell my mum and Olivia whilst I was highlighting my mum's hair. The irony of that sentence! They were both more surprised than I expected, and both burst into tears. My mum said at the time that she wasn't crying because I was gay; it was just that she couldn't imagine how lonely it must have been to go through it on my own. I still think it was because she was disappointed, or that I'd let her down. I remember some of the throw away comments that both my mum and sister used to make – things that would make me think that I'd never be able to come out to them without them hating me; the eighties were a pretty tough time in that respect. But as the years have passed, I do now believe that Mum and Olivia have accepted it. I think I still have a little way to fully accept myself. The thought of counselling popped into my head again and I wondered when I'd feel ready to face up to all of this, just as *I'm Coming Out* came on. I smiled and glanced at Mum as I turned it up.

"I used to love this one!" she said, smiling back oblivious to the resonance that song had.

It was just after 1pm as we arrived at Olivia's house in Ipswich. Like me, she also lived in a new build house that they'd moved to a couple of years ago, in the district of Great Blakenham. Their house was on a corner, which gave them a nice big plot, but it always made parking a little awkward. I found a space just in front of Daniel's Audi on the road outside. Louise opened the front door as we got out of the car.

"Hi Nanny and Uncle!"

"Hi Louise! How are you? You've grown a lot since I last saw you," I exclaimed. It was true – she had shot up. Her long dark hair danced around as she came running out to greet us with her trademark cheeky smile.

"I'm fine, thank you Uncle!"

"That's good! Hi Liv, you OK?"

"Yes, I'm good thanks. How was the journey?" Olivia had come to the door and looked a little tired but in general appeared to be in good spirits. She'd tied her hair back and her make-up was simple and natural. She was dressed casually in a summery dress.

"It was fine, wasn't it, mum? The traffic wasn't bad for a Saturday afternoon!"

We came into the house, took off our shoes and were ushered into the living room where Louise immediately wanted to show us something on the tv from YouTube. Daniel came down the stairs and said his hellos and we all took a seat on the sofas.

"Right, let me get you some drinks – what would you like?" Olivia took the order of coffees, teas and an orange juice for Louise and wandered out to the kitchen.

"I'll just see if she needs a hand." I said as I got to my feet and followed her. I had the death certificate in my pocket, and I put my hand into my jeans to hold on to it.

"You OK?" Olivia looked at me quizzically as I arrived in the kitchen. Admittedly I never helped her with drinks before. She'd put the kettle on and was taking some mugs out of the cupboard.

"Yes – I'm fine… I've erm, I've got some information about Dad." I walked closer to her and she stopped what she was doing and looked at me, eyes wide and mouth open.

"Have you? Have you *found* him?" She sounded dumbfounded, no doubt reacting to my concerned expression.

"No… I've got… I've found a death certificate for him."

"Oh my god! Really? What…" She stopped short of asking the question she was going to ask and looked thoughtfully at me, slightly frowning with confusion.

"He died in 2016," I said quietly. "And he had Motor Neurone Disease."

"Oh dear… that's not nice."

"Are you alright? I know it's a lot to take in."

Before Olivia could answer, Louise ran out into the kitchen.

"My granddad has died," she proclaimed, matter-of-factly.

"What? Were you listening to us?" I asked her, a little annoyed at the interruption.

"No, Nanny has just told Daddy."

I rolled my eyes as my mum and Daniel appeared at the entrance of the kitchen.

"Mum!"

"Look, all I said to Daniel was that my husband had died and that's what you were telling Olivia. I didn't think Louise would piece it together." My mum looked desperately apologetic. "But she's so clever she understood exactly!" Louise beamed.

"OK, well we all know now," I smiled, bemused at the chaos, but I was admittedly relieved that there hadn't been any tears or drama so far. I looked at Olivia again. "I've got the death certificate with me if you want to see it?"

I handed the document to Olivia as she waited for the kettle to boil and she reviewed it carefully in silence. She put it on the worktop as she poured the boiling water, without taking her eyes off it. We traipsed back to the living room with our drinks and took our seats once more.

"What a shock. I wasn't expecting you to tell me *that* today." Olivia was looking at the document again.

"Are you ok?"

"Yes, I think so." It struck me that I'd had a few days to get my head around it and it was something I'd been thinking about for ages and I'd been actively looking for, but Olivia hadn't had any prior warning so I did feel for her, and could see she was consumed with her thoughts. "I can't believe he was still with Siobhan. She was such a *bitch*!"

"Yes, I know. But she stayed with him all through his illness. Regardless of how long he had it, it couldn't have been easy."

"So, he must have died at home? Not in a hospital?"

"With terminal illnesses I think people are sometimes transferred home if they want familiar surroundings, provided they have the care they need." I thought back to a friend's parent who'd died from terminal cancer and how they were given palliative care when they were moved back home to spend their last days there with their loved ones. How comforting it had been for them not to be in hospital with strangers, but surrounded by the people they loved in the home they could relax in.

"If we'd known, we could have helped out – if I could have helped in any way I would've done," said my mum. Olivia and I both stared at her.

"Really?" said Olivia. We exchanged glances, both shocked at this declaration.

"Yes! I'd hate to have seen anyone go through such a difficult time – not that she'd accept my help. Oh, I bet she would have hated it if I had turned up and offered any assistance at all!" Mum grimaced. "She was quite a woman and she resented me."

"She wasn't particularly keen on *any* of us," I added.

"No, but she felt threatened by me. I remember your dad telling me that there was this young girl who kept following him around and wouldn't leave him alone. I think he was telling me in a round-about way that this was my last chance to get back with him, but I'd already moved on and so I said to him: 'Good for you! Why don't you take her out if you like her?' And, so he did, but I think she knew, to begin with at least, that he still loved me."

"I remember the row on the front doorstep – that was the first time I saw how nasty she was," I said.

"And do you know what that was all about?" My mum puffed herself up, preparing to enlighten us all. "One afternoon, when your dad was taking you out for the day, he also knew I was going out to the shops, so he drove round the block and waited until I'd left, and then came back and let you all in. He still had a key because at that time we were on good terms. He showed Siobhan around the house and made you all a cup of tea and then took you out somewhere. When he dropped you off, he told me that Siobhan liked the house and wanted to move in – meaning that we would have to move out!"

"What? That's ridiculous!" I said. Olivia was less shocked but shook her head none the less.

"I know," Mum continued. "It caused a terrible argument on the doorstep in front of all the neighbours – what must they have thought – and I remember her pushing the conversation. She kept saying: 'this is *his* house!' and I was saying: 'No, this is *our* house – it's half mine too – my name is on the deeds as well!'" I remembered this so well but at the time I had no idea what the row was about. Siobhan certainly had some front. "In the end it caused us to have to put the house up for sale, and then we moved in with Alf in Canvey." I went cold at the thought of that time again. It was such an unsettling period. "Your dad changed so much when she came on the scene. He was always so easy going and carefree, but she took him over and manipulated him. I just wish he'd have been a bit stronger."

"Mum, Siobhan was a lot younger than Dad, wasn't she?" I asked, "Do know what the age difference was?"

"Ooh, I think she was about ten years younger than your dad, so she'd be mid-sixties now I think?" Mum made a face again. "Yes, she was the younger woman. Slim, long brown hair, pouty lips..." Olivia and I exchanged glances again. Mum had left *him*; not the other way round. Mum seemed to have a tendency to be the victim in so many situations where she really wasn't.

Olivia had made us a nice sandwich lunch with salad and crisps on the side and we moved to the kitchen diner to enjoy it. Conversation still centred around Dad but became a little more light-hearted.

"I know it's awful, but I'll always remember the moment your dad left," said my mum as she looked at me with a wry smile. "Your reaction was priceless! You looked at me distraught and said: *'Who's going to clean out the guinea pigs now?'* And I said, 'well if that's all we've got to worry about I'm sure we'll be fine!'"

The subtle sound of laughter was a welcome relief from the seriousness of what had been discussed earlier. We reminisced about the metallic brown car he had – a Triumph Princess, which was his pride and joy and was the envy of the street. It was so seventies, but at the time, the height of class and sophistication.

"Do you remember when we were at the dinner table and you said that you didn't want your mash and you gave it to Dad to finish off?" I looked at Olivia as she began to giggle. Such a random thing to pop into my head, but she knew exactly what I was about to say. "And when he'd finished the last mouthful, you told him that you'd just spat it all out!"

We both collapsed in peals of laughter, much to the puzzlement of Mum, Daniel and Louise. It had felt good to talk things through with Olivia and Mum openly and honestly, probably for the first time as adults. There was still some pain hidden away and I still had a lot of unanswered questions, but for now they could wait for another day.

Conversation moved to my birthday, which was coming up on 10th October. I never liked my birthday and always resisted a fuss, but the tradition had been to go to a local pub for a drink and some lunch, so that was the compromise. We arranged that Olivia and co would come down to us on Saturday 12th October and we'd have lunch in the Horse and Groom, just outside Chelmsford.

The day after seeing Olivia and the family I had nothing planned and felt fidgety and restless. My dad was again occupying my thoughts and I once more studied the death certificate looking for more answers that it wasn't able to provide. I suddenly wanted to know what his house looked like. I wanted to picture where he lived and died; where he'd been hiding all those years. I googled the address and it immediately brought up a link for Zoopla, which I clicked on. As I navigated through, I saw that the last time the house was sold was January 1996. It had been bought for £95,000 and was now worth approximately £490,000.   It was a four-bedroom detached house. *That was a big house for two people to live in.* Could there be a mistake? I checked again and saw that I definitely had the correct address. 1996 was the year before I moved out into my flat and house prices were very low then. This also appeared to show that Siobhan still lived there; she hadn't moved to a new house after he'd died. I imagined how empty a big four-bedroom house must be after losing your partner after so many years and felt a pang of sympathy for her. She may have moved out and had let it to tenants? It was a possibility, I guess.

I suddenly wondered whether they had children together. My dad was 39 or 40 when I last saw him, so it wasn't out of the question. I felt a twinge of sadness at the thought of him with other children, having lovingly raising them whilst knowing we still existed without his love.

After Zoopla, I looked on Google Street View to see what the house looked like. For some reason I couldn't line up the right house. It showed number 21 in Google on the graphics, despite me entering the correct address, and when I moved along the street I just got lost. After about half an hour of trying this, I gave up and then thought about driving there to see if for myself. I toyed with the idea for a few minutes; it was around 6.45 and it would still light for another hour or so. I'd got the postcode from Google already, so I kept it on my phone as I went downstairs and opened the internal door to my garage. I got in my car, started the engine and entered the post code into the sat nav system. It estimated 24 minutes to get to the house. *He was only ever 24 minutes away.* I reversed out of my garage and headed towards the city centre where I could join the A130 and drive to Canvey Island.

My heart was beating slightly faster as nerves began to set in, although I wasn't entirely sure why. I was clear that I didn't want to see Siobhan and prayed that there wouldn't be a bizarre coincidence of me arriving outside her house just as she'd decided to go for a walk.

I hadn't really taken any notice of the journey or where I'd driven and before I knew it, I was only a few minutes away. The next turning on the right would be Crescent Drive. I could see the road approaching and then smoothly turned into it. *I was now in my dad's road.* I slowly drove halfway down, trying to see the house numbers but unable to make any out. It was overcast and the sun was low, not quite twilight but near enough. The streetlights were just beginning to come on, pink initially before morphing into the familiar orange glow. I pulled up on the left and parked, taking a deep breath as I got out of my car, and walked silently along the pavement. It was a noticeably quiet area with just a distant hum of the occasional car passing from the road I'd just come from. Number 45; number 43... a few houses along... number 39 – here it is: Number 37. It was a surreal feeling. So, this is where he'd lived; all those years of wondering where he was, and this is where he'd been all that time. It was a large, detached house, with an open arched porch over the front door in the centre of the house with a matching arch over the entrance to the garage on the right.   I could see net curtains hanging in the windows obscuring any view of the inside, although it looked as though curtains had been drawn anyway. Once upon a time it looked like it could have been a happy family home. I wondered what ghosts hid behind the walls; what memories lurked within the house over the past twenty years or so. The front garden was overgrown with long grass and unkempt bushes bordering the pavement. A towering rosebush dominated the left side of the garden, branches leaning down precariously, threatening to catch any passers-by that came too close. The front door was muted from dirt that had accumulated over the years. It had a foreboding look about it, no doubt exacerbated because of the fading light.

The house was in darkness apart from one window upstairs in the middle of the house, which was bathed in soft pink light from the curtains that had been pulled. So that was where Siobhan was? In that room, upstairs on her own? I pictured my dad in the front garden, mowing the lawn like he used to do before he left; it didn't look as if anyone had done any gardening for a long time. I only lingered for a few minutes, not wanting to look suspicious or draw attention from Siobhan or any of her neighbours. I looked around briefly before I turned and walked back to my car.

I drove back home unable to escape the anticlimactic feeling, wondering if seeing his house would satisfy my curiosity and stop the persisting questions. I wasn't sure it was, although I didn't know what else would, and wondered whether I just needed time to process everything.

I arrived home and parked in my garage. I glanced down and saw my phone was flashing from a message I'd received. It was from Olivia.

So why am I now itching to go and see
Dad's house? Mixed emotions, head all
over the place!

I chuckled to myself, baffled by the way our minds both
worked. I quickly responded:

Time for a quick chat?

She picked up the phone within half a ring.
"Hey, you ok? I asked.
"Yes. I think so. I guess it's all just sinking in now. I've
been up and down all day, one moment not really thinking
much about it, another moment I've been quite emotional.
I've driven poor Danny mad!"
"If ever you want to talk about it please call me." I
meant it.
"Yes, I will. Thankyou."
"Yesterday really helped me to talk it through."
"Aww, I'm pleased. In a weird way it was a really nice
day. It was lovely to see you and Mum, but it felt good to talk
in depth about all of this."
We were only on the phone for about 15 minutes as
Olivia had to get dinner ready, but she exclaimed when I told
her where I'd just been.
"Look, you don't have to keep on doing everything
yourself," she said. "I'm happy to come along with you so that
you're not on your own."
She listened with interest as I described the house. "If
you wanted, we could go back, and you could see it?"
"No, it's ok. There's a part of me that is really curious
and another part where I don't know whether I want to find
out anymore." She paused. "Are you going to do anything
else?"

"I don't know. I'm not sure what I want to do yet. I was thinking of writing to Siobhan but I... I don't know."

"I spoke to Mum earlier and I think she's worried that you'll get in contact with her."

"What did she say?"

"I think she's just worried that you'll get hurt more than anything else."

"I wished she'd speak to me about this! What do you think?"

"Like I said, you don't have to do this on your own, but I guess it's up to you."

The next week or so I resisted the urge to do anything more regarding my dad and just took time to process and think things through. I didn't want to rush into anything and regret it. Work was busy, which was a helpful distraction and I caught up with friends and old work colleagues for after work drinks a few times. Eventually I decided that I still had enough curiosity to do a bit more digging, and I conceded that the only way of finding out any more information was through Siobhan. I talked to Olivia about this, but to avoid unnecessary worry from Mum, I chose not to say anything to her (just yet, anyway).

I drafted a letter, which I rewrote a few times; in the end I thought I'd keep it to the point and make an initial enquiry, and depending on whether she'd respond we could take it from there. I thought the easiest way would be to meet up and have a conversation, rather than send her a barrage of questions, although I hesitated about suggesting this. Did I really want to meet up with her? I still wasn't 100% sure. I was also very mindful of not upsetting her and wanted to reiterate that I didn't want to cause any trouble. I knew I was overthinking It, so I printed the letter out at work and read it for the final time:

Dear Siobhan

My name is Colin and I'm James's son. I recently found out that James passed away in 2016, which after a period of reflection has left me wanting to find out more about his life since I last saw him.

I reflected on the part promising not to turn up at her door unannounced, bearing in mind the road trip the other weekend. However, I still wanted to provide reassurance and not cause any unnecessary panic. I put the letter in an envelope and carefully sealed it. Even as I was doing this a rush of adrenalin coursed through my body and I hoped to God that I'd get a response – a positive response at that; although the doubts about meeting up with her still persisted. I posted the letter in the post box just outside my office building as I left for the evening and then walked back to Liverpool Street station.

In a way, the fact that I'd sent a letter to Siobhan stopped my head whirling; maybe because I'd done all that I could up to that point and, I suppose, I wasn't convinced I'd get a reply from her. I gave her a way out of not responding so it was in her hands now. The following day I did wonder if she'd received my letter and imagined her shock as she opened it, but then bizarrely, didn't really think that much about it. That weekend I was away with the friends I'd gone to Greece with which was wonderful. We'd got the train to Winchester on Friday evening and were staying in a beautiful cottage on a quiet country lane. It was a weekend of laughter, long walks, country pubs, playing cards and forgetting about current or past troubles. Just what I needed!

I'd arrived home and saw an envelope on the mat. I picked it up curiously. The address was written in biro, but in dramatic, almost calligraphic writing. I saw that it was addressed to Mr C. E. Walters and I know I didn't use my middle name when writing to Siobhan. It couldn't be from her already! It had only been a few days. I opened it carefully as I walked towards the kitchen before I even took my coat off.

Dear Colin

Thank you for your letter. You say that you would like to know about James's life since you last saw him. I am more than willing to answer any questions you may have, but I don't feel that it would be right for us to meet. I just cannot imagine meeting you after all this time, without James by my side.

I hope that you can understand, but as I said I am more than willing to answer any questions you may have. Just send me the questions and I will do my very best to answer.

Best wishes for Thursday,

Siobhan

I read her letter twice and then paused before I read it a third time. She had responded. She had responded - and she was willing to answer questions about my dad! I felt initial relief that we weren't going to meet after all, but I suddenly felt that the undefinable closure I was looking for was now within reach and my heart soared. She also knew my middle initial – and *'best wishes for Thursday'* – my birthday was Thursday! How did she know my birthday? Maybe this wouldn't be such a sad ending after all.

I called Olivia and read the letter to her. She reacted excitedly and said that this was the first time she'd ever felt positive about it. I was so happy that I'd decided to reach out to Siobhan after the endless deliberating. I asked if Olivia had any questions that she'd like me to include in my reply, but her mind had gone blank and she couldn't think of anything. I suggested we meet up the following week to go through it and she agreed. We set a date for Tuesday 15th October. We were already seeing each other on Saturday but as Mum didn't know about the letter, it wouldn't have been appropriate to discuss it then. After I put the phone down, I drafted a response to Siobhan, which took all of ten minutes.

I saw Jane on Sunday and showed her Siobhan's letter. She studied it carefully.

"Do you think she's offering an olive branch?" she asked.

"I don't know. I guess? There's no animosity there is there? And for her to wish me happy birthday is…." I struggled to find the words.

"I bet your dad did have regrets and the fact that she was able to respond so quickly and know your middle initial and your birthday shows that you were not forgotten about. They probably raised a toast to you and your sister every birthday and Christmas!"

"Do you think so?" I had such a warm positive feeling about this now.

"Yeah, I do." She read the letter again. "She does come across a little panicked, though. Don't you think?"

"What do you mean?"

"Well, she's repeated herself a couple of times, reiterating that she's willing to answer any questions but I suppose not wanting to meet up."

"To be honest, I'm more relieved than disappointed at that myself."

"So, what are you going to ask her?"

<u>Tuesday 15th October 2019</u>

I'd left work a little early and arrived back in Chelmsford just after 6pm. The nights were really drawing in and I noticed how dark it already was. I'd parked in Chelmsford city centre near to the station, so I walked to my car, bathed in the orange glow of the streetlights, and started my drive to Ipswich. Rush hour traffic in Chelmsford was notoriously bad so I took my time, listening to Drive Time with Sara Cox on Radio 2, and smiled, looking forward to the discussion with Olivia. On Saturday the Dad Subject had been touched upon, but didn't dominate the conversation. Mum seemed relaxed and happy that the topic appeared to be closed and I did feel ever so slightly guilty going behind her back now and not telling her the latest developments. But I knew what she was like and she'd drive herself (and the rest of us) mad, worrying about it and wondering what would happen next.

I arrived at Olivia's house just after 7pm and parked outside. Olivia appeared at the door having seen me pull up. She got in the passenger side and the scent of her Marc Jacobs perfume flooded the car. Louise and Daniel waved us off enthusiastically.

"You look nice," I said, genuinely meaning it. It wasn't often I went out for a drink with Olivia now, not that we lived a million miles away from each other, but we hardly ever saw each other during the week and at weekends it was always during the day. She had done her makeup and was wearing a nice elegant dress with a smart leather jacket.

"Thanks." She smiled, enjoying the compliment.

"Where shall we go? I'm starving so somewhere that does good food."

Olivia suggested The Chequers which was a short drive away and we set off with Olivia directing me. We arrived within about 10 minutes and quickly found a table. It was typically quiet for a Tuesday evening and the only other punters were old men propping up the bar, and a couple maybe on a first date in the corner. It was a nice, traditional looking pub and had a good feel to it. After I got us some drinks and ordered food, I took out the draft of the letter I'd written and gave it to Olivia to read. She took it and studied it carefully.

"I think you've covered everything I wanted to know..." she said slowly as she read it for a second time. "What do you think she'll come back with?"

"Who knows? I'm hoping it will be positive and friendly. She's said she'll answer anything we want her to. How are you feeling about it all?"

"Much better than when we all found out about it. I'm glad Mum doesn't know about this – you can imagine what she'd be like!" She laughed, rolling her eyes. "She just makes everything about her. I couldn't believe it when she said she'd want to help out if she'd known about Dad's illness! At the end of it all she hated him!"

"I know. It's all very strange," I agreed. "I think she's forgetting the affair she had – she wasn't exactly blameless herself! Well, we don't have to say anything to Mum just yet, if at all, I suppose." We were briefly interrupted as our food was brought out. I'd ordered scampi and chips and Olivia had ordered lasagne with a side salad. Good solid pub grub!

In between mouthfuls, Olivia reviewed the letter again and we tweaked a few words here and there. I was very conscious of taking out any language that could be interpreted as confrontational and I switched a few things around to make it read a bit better.

"I'll print it out at work tomorrow and send it off to her," I said with an optimistic smile. "Hopefully, she'll reply soon, and then I guess that will be it." Olivia nodded and smiled. "How are things with Kirstie? Any better?"

The smile turned to a grimace. "She's just trying to cause trouble, now. She complained to her mum that me and Danny are ganging up on her! Can you believe that? She's so manipulative. So, Danny's been on the phone to the mother, trying to convince her that it's Kirstie was out of line, but at the end of the day, she's his daughter and he loves her despite all the shit she causes." Olivia took a large sip from her wine glass. "Anyway, I don't want to talk about her anymore!"

The evening passed quickly and enjoyably. I thought we should do this more often and not just when we have to talk about family matters. It was nice to catch up, just the two of us like we used to many years ago. I dropped Olivia off around 10.30 and got home about 11.30.

<u>**Wednesday 16th October 2019**</u>

The following day I made the changes to the letter that Olivia and I had discussed last night and printed it out. I gave it a final read before I sealed it in the envelope:

Dear Siobhan

Many thanks for your letter and thanks so much for responding so quickly. I can imagine that receiving my first letter must have come as a shock and I completely understand and respect your request not to meet face to face.

One of the reasons I wanted to meet up was because the questions in my head were difficult for me to articulate in a letter and maybe a conversation would have been easier – but below is my attempt. I am grateful for any answers you are comfortable providing; please don't feel under any pressure to answer anything you don't want to, and apologies if there's anything here that makes you feel uncomfortable – this is absolutely not my intention.

Firstly, I just want to know that he had a good life and you were happy together. He was always in my mind and I have always wondered what happened after he said goodbye. Do you have a photo of him that you would be happy to send me?

I guess you didn't marry from seeing your surname. Did you ever have children?

When I saw the cause of his death on the death certificate this came as a huge shock. Did he have good health for most of his life? How long did he have MND? Do you know how this was caused? Did he suffer for a long period? Did you have support to care for him?

One thing that took me by surprise was when receiving your letter was the fact that you used my middle initial on the envelope, as well as you remembering my birthday, the assumption that I had was after we last saw him, he didn't look back (in every sense), but seeing you use this information has made me question this. Did he ever talk about us? Do you think he ever thought about us?

Finally, was he (and are you) in touch with his family? By that I mean his brother Harry and his sister Deb.

Those are all the questions I have for the moment. As I stated before, please only respond with what you feel comfortable answering.

Thanks again and best wishes,

Colin

As I read it for a final time, I lingered on the part about whether he ever talked about us and whether he may have thought about us. This was the most difficult thing to articulate and something I deliberated most about whether I should include or not. But at the end of the day, it's something I wanted to know – it was actually something I *needed* to know, and the main reason I was writing the letter. I posted it during my lunch break and felt a positive rush of anticipation as the envelope left my fingers and dropped into the post box. I couldn't wait for Siobhan's reply, but it turned out to be a longer wait than anticipated.

Three weeks had passed and still nothing had arrived in the post. I came home every day, eager to see a brown envelope on my mat but I was always left disappointed and I wondered what the reason for the delay could be. I was round Jane's one evening and was discussing it with her.

"Give it time. It might be that it's difficult for her to recall some of the memories." Jane paused as she considered another theory. "It might even be that she's contacted your aunt and your uncle and she's waiting on *them* before she replies to you."

I hadn't considered this and actually, that could be a valid reason for the wait. I nodded in support, excited, but at the same time apprehensive at the prospect of reconnecting with Uncle Harry and Aunty Deb. Back in the day, we were quite close with Harry, especially. He was always kind and seemed to look forward to seeing us and we used to have so such fun with his daughter Abigail, who was a similar age to us.

"In your letter, you didn't ask about the Will, did you?"

"No. I deliberately didn't mention anything about that. I mean, it's been three and a half years; all of that would have been settled long ago and there was nothing in her first letter to suggest we were left anything, so it didn't really cross my mind to do that."

"I wonder if she thinks you're fishing for information and want to make a claim on the estate?"

"I don't think I *could* do that, could I?"

"I'm not sure. I know that relatives can contest Wills even after they have been settled. I don't know. Will you chase her up if you don't get a reply soon? I suppose it's a bit delicate...?"

"I had already thought about that. I was thinking of waiting until December and then I'd send her a Christmas card with a small message wishing her a merry Christmas and that I'd love to hear back from her whenever she had time to reply, or something like that."

"Yes, that sounds like it could work. Hopefully you'll get something back soon though!"

At work the following day, I thought about Jane's comment about Dad's Will and wondered if I could get a copy of it. In between meetings, I googled 'how to get a copy of a Will'. The first link that came up was a link to a government website titled *Search probate records for documents and wills (England and Wales)*. I clicked on this. The search was surprisingly simple; it just required the surname of the person who died and the year of death. It then brought up a list of people matching that criteria, whose Wills you could order. I was surprised how easy and straight forward this was and amazed at how publicly available this information could be. There were 63 entries for the surname Walters and year of death 2016, but as I scrolled, Dad's name wasn't listed. I went through it again, slower this time, but still no entry for Dad. I clicked on the Advanced Search link, which enabled more detail to be entered to narrow the search. Again, nothing for my dad. I searched under 2015 and 2017 in case there had been an administrative error. Still nothing turned up. I was baffled; he must have had a Will. *Unless* he transferred everything to Siobhan's name before he died?

I quickly googled the land registry website. After a few clicks, just entering the house number and postcode gave me the option of ordering a Title Register, a Title Plan and a Flood Risk Indicator Result. I clicked on the Title Register option, which after having to enter my name and address, then prompted me to enter my credit card details to pay £3 for the document. And then it was there to download. I opened it and saw to my amazement that the registered owner was my dad. No-one else was listed. *The house was still in his sole name.*

I sat back, stunned that Dad's estate had never been dealt with. What could be the reason for this? He must have had a Will, but it had been three and a half years, and nothing had been done. Maybe he didn't have a Will? But *he had a terminal illness*, so it's not as if he didn't have time to prepare. Even when he was close to death and completely incapacitated, something could have been sorted for him. And why had he and Siobhan not married? Surely all of this could have been resolved if they'd just had a quick ceremony to make them legally wed. None of it made any sense, but then this had to be the reason that Siobhan hadn't responded to my letter. Jane was right – she thought I was going after the estate!

I quickly googled intestacy rules. Another government website came up. A couple of questions asking if the deceased had a living spouse and living children – I answered "no" to spouse as I assumed that he hadn't married Siobhan – and the answer came back unequivocally: *The estate is shared equally between the children or their descendants.* I checked Zoopla again, and again saw that the house was estimated to be valued at £490,000. That could be a nice little nest egg.

When I got home from work, I'd had time to think this through a little on the train and called Olivia to let her know about the latest development.

"Has she responded?" she asked excitedly.

"No, not yet – but there is a bit of a twist that I didn't see coming!"

I explained what I'd found out to Olivia and what the potential implications were.

"So, we're in for a windfall!" Olivia sounded incredulous.

"Well, maybe," I said cautiously. "We shouldn't jump to conclusions just yet – we don't know if they did have children together, so anything would be split equally between us all. But also, you have to consider that she stayed with him for 35 years, and I guess cared for him throughout his illness so, depending on what happens, I think we should think of this to be our retirement fund. I think we should allow Siobhan to continue to live there for the rest of her life, and then when she dies, we can sell it or let it out, or do whatever we want with it."

Olivia paused, reflecting on my suggestion. "She didn't consider *us*, though did she? And do you really want to be tied to her for *the rest of her life?* She's a nasty piece of work and I think we should kick her out and sell up."

I was shocked at the brutality of Olivia's reaction. "I get what you're saying, but at the end of the day, it was his decision to not see us and to do what he did. OK – she may have influenced that, but it doesn't take away the responsibility *he* had." I hesitated. "Think of Kirstie. If you could take action to make sure that Kirstie was cut out of your lives, I'm sure you'd do it."

"Oh, that's different."

"Why is it different? It's only different because you have a different perspective on it. It's all the same really. Look, we don't have to do anything about it now and I don't want to rush into anything just yet anyway, especially with Christmas coming up. I would hate to do anything that we would regret later so I think we should let this all sink in and then maybe in the new year we can decide what to do."

I was still a little shocked at Olivia's reaction and hoped that after the news had sunk in, she'd calm down and start to think a little more rationally about it all. I expected that she would eventually, but she might need a little more convincing before she did. I was just so conscious of not doing anything rash that we would both come to regret.

I had a quiet weekend planned, which was the first one since my holiday and I was actually looking forward to not doing that much. Autumn was in full flow and the leaves had turned to beautiful golden, red and orange colours; the air was fresh and although the nights were drawing in and the mornings were beginning to get darker, I think this was my favourite season. This year, all records had been broken for how hot the summer had been, so the coolness in the air was a welcome change, although October had been pretty wet so far with torrential rain on most days. However, on Saturday, it was a nice day and the sun was out so I decided to go for a long walk, which always helped clear my head. I was lucky to live in an area that had so much beautiful countryside to explore, however I was also in the middle of an expanding housing development and many of the walking routes I'd enjoyed had turned slowly into building sites. It was a terrible shame, but at the same time I acknowledged that I was part of the problem, having bought one of the houses a few years before. Having said that, Countryside, the building developer, had planned lots of green open space, no doubt due to planning restrictions, so it wasn't all bad. But nothing could beat some of the views of the unspoilt rolling fields and meadows that were now making way for diggers and foundations to be laid.

White clouds were moving doggedly across the blue sky as I walked down a new route I'd recently stumbled upon, an area that was relatively unspoilt, for now anyway, which led to a small forest emblazoned in stunning autumnal colours. I then crossed a narrow babbling river, leading through a meadow with long grass and into a field where cows were grazing. It was wonderful and with the wind in my face I filled my lungs with the fresh air, instantly feeling better. In my head I went through everything I'd found out so far about

Dad. I still hoped that Siobhan would write back to me, but after my discovery earlier this week, I had my doubts whether she would now. I was confused as to why she responded to my first letter when I gave her a pretty good get-out clause. If she'd chosen not to reply, I might not have thought that much more about it and that could have been the end of it. But then I suppose I'd still have lots of questions and maybe I'd have done more digging; who knows really? I didn't feel any nearer to getting closure at the moment and the most recent development about the ownership of the house and the apparent absence of a Will made me apprehensive at what the next steps could or should be. I thought back to Olivia and completely understood her position. Siobhan was the reason we didn't have a dad growing up; Siobhan was the reason we struggled so much financially, and we owed her nothing. And maybe Olivia thought that the house would be a back payment for all the missed maintenance payments that we should have had as children. From my perspective, I was still very much aware of how difficult it must have been for Siobhan to have provided care for him during his illness. Admittedly I had no idea how involved Siobhan was, but the fact that he was in the house when he died implied that she had more of a hands-on approach. Her letter also felt warm and genuine, albeit slightly panicked, but who wouldn't be shocked to receive a letter like the one I'd sent out of the blue? I was still very conscious of not doing anything that I'd later look back on and regret. It was such a difficult and contentious subject, but I hoped that we'd find a compromise at some point soon.

I thought about Dad's family and wondered what their reaction would have been when he'd told them that we were out of the picture, never to return again. Surely, they would have asked questions and challenged him on this decision? I'd have thought that my nan would have had a few choice words to say about it and I'd have hoped my Uncle Harry would have been able to persuade or influence Dad in some way? Nothing made sense and I accepted that I would probably not get the answers I craved so much.

It was raining. I left work early to get back to Chelmsford as fast as I could, half running through Devonshire Square to get to Liverpool Street station. I didn't have an umbrella and I was trying to weave in and out of the meandering commuters that all did have umbrellas. I'd come home last night to a red and white card from the post office, notifying me that they'd tried to deliver a recorded delivery letter. It was addressed to Mr C E Walters. It *had* to be from Siobhan – no one else addressed anything to me by that name. By the time I'd got in last night, it was too late to collect it, so I'd taken the card to work with me that morning with a view to drive to the collection office and pick it up when I got off the train. I was nervous and excited at the same time and I'd messaged Olivia to let her know that a potential reply was waiting. She'd responded positively and asked me to promise to call her as soon as I'd received it, which I agreed to do.

By the time I got off the train, it had stopped raining thankfully. The streets glistened under the glow of the streetlights. I rushed to my car and navigated the busy rush-hour roads to the collection office. Having parked, I took my place in the queue and eventually I was served. I was handed an A4 envelope which had the familiar extravagant writing on it – *It was from her!* – and it felt as though it was padded with cardboard. I raced back to my car and turned on the internal light. I didn't want to wait until I got home to see what she'd sent me.

I tore open the envelope eagerly and took out the contents. There were two sheets of cardboard to keep the package flat and Siobhan had written a letter, of which there were two copies. But she had also sent some pictures! Two A4 sheets of paper displayed colour photocopied pictures of my dad, three pictures on each sheet of paper. There were two copies of these too. I studied them carefully, feeling all kinds of emotions. It was strange and bittersweet for me to see pictures of Dad, after all these years, some of him as I remember him; some of him as an older man. I could see the family resemblance immediately – I definitely had his mouth and chin and, unusually as he got older, I could see that we had the same shaped face overall. Aside from the fact that he had dark hair and my colouring was slightly fairer, we looked very similar. There was one of him dressed in a tuxedo, looking back over his shoulder, trying to pull off a suave expression; others were more relaxed and casual. One of him chilling on the sofa, another holding a huge bouquet of flowers in a very eighties styled living room. I recognised his smile, confident and self-assured, completely as ease with himself, as if he didn't have a care in the world. I found myself envious of him, not knowing the hardships we'd endured; blissfully ignorant, without worrying about whether we were ok. But then I wondered how happy he really was; whether the smiles were masking any pain or regret; whether he genuinely lived a blissful life without worry or concern. He looked generally content in every picture, which I guess most people do if they're having their photo taken. It was interesting that each picture was only of him and didn't feature Siobhan in any of them. I wondered how recent the pictures of him as an older man were. The one where he looked oldest, he was wearing glasses, his hair was short with flecks of grey. He was half smiling, but certainly not as carefree as the earlier shots. I wondered whether this would have been one of the last pictures of him before his illness took hold.

I pulled my eyes away from the pictures and picked up Siobhan's letter, my heart filled with anticipation.

Dear Colin

After I received your letter, I dug out some old documents and found your full name and D.O.B. Please don't read more into it than that. I'm sorry if you thought otherwise.

You asked if James ever looked back after that last meeting. I have to say when he came out of the office and got into the car, he was furious that instead of the three of you being in the waiting room, you had already gone into the welfare officer's room before he had even arrived. James saw this as you once again going behind his back and he just snapped. Whether it was done to antagonise him or not, for James it was the last straw.

I stopped reading, jarred by the bluntness of Siobhan's revelations. He never thought of us or talked about us? He clearly never looked back or regretted anything about what he did? And it seemed that all of this was because we went into a room without waiting for him? *We were children and we did what we were told.* My heart had stopped as her words hit me like punch in the stomach.

He came out of that meeting a different person. From then on, instead of taking advice from his solicitor he told her exactly what he wanted done before the case moved to the courts. I'm not sure how much you know about the planned hearing, but due to everything James had discovered, it made him doubt every single thing about his marriage, from day one.

As for James's sister, Deb died in 2002 from pancreatic cancer. James's mother died from the same illness. As far as I know his brother is still alive since mid-2016. For any update I can only suggest you contact his wife, Amanda. I do remember that he was diabetic.

I don't know if you remember Harry's wife/partner Christine. She died very young. She was the mother of Harry's three sons. After Christine died, Harry and Amanda married and Amanda devoted herself to raising the three boys as her own, despite having her own health problems.

James was diagnosed with MND in late 2004, after months of us being told by our GP and consultant that his symptoms were caused by migraines. He spent three weeks in hospital and then discharged himself when the consultant didn't arrive when he said he would, to sign for him to go home. So, he signed himself out and we got a cab and went home. He was only willing to go back for check-ups. I believe it was because James was so strong that he was able to speak, eat and drink as normal until the end. He was determined to stay with me for as long as possible. James knew that no matter what he needed I would be by his side 24 hours a day.

I sat in my car, cold and numb at how brutal Siobhan had been. I'd made such an effort to not upset or offend her and she had done nothing to spare my feelings; if anything, it felt like she'd intentionally gone out of her way to upset me. Why focus on the moments after the meeting at the welfare office? I expected to hear about hobbies they'd shared; holidays they'd been on, why they chose to live in Canvey and how they decorated the house. Instead, it was a cheap Mills and Boon account of how much in love they were without any substance, but laced with bitterness – why was she still bitter and resentful after 35 years of living her best life? Even the part about his only regret ever being not meeting her twelve years earlier – my mum and dad were married for twelve years; such a passive aggressive and unnecessary detail to include. He had no regrets about anything else he'd done? If anything, he wanted to erase the part of his life that included me and Olivia? The hurt I felt was almost a physical pain in my chest and I held myself tight, trying to find some comfort. I felt so incredibly foolish at placing all my faith in the belief that she could have come back with anything positive that could help with closure or healing the wounds of the past. I felt like the rejected 9-year-old child all over again. I *hated* her in that moment, more than I can remember hating anyone or anything. It took everything for me not to rip her fucking letter into thousands of pieces.

I jumped as my phone buzzed – it was a message from Olivia:

```
So?  Did you get it?  Can't wait to hear
what she's said! X
```

My heart plummeted as I thought about Olivia, waiting eagerly by the phone, about to be as disappointed and crushed as I was feeling. *But this was all because of me; she hadn't asked for any of this.* I drove home without responding to her message and when I got in, I read the letter again a couple of times before I called her, devastated and angry in equal measure. I took a deep breath.

"Hey, you OK?" I asked as she picked up the phone.

"Yes, I'm good. Did you get it?" She sounded cautiously excited.

"Yeah. I've got it. Look, it's not the nicest of letters, Liv. Do you want me to read it to you?"

There was silence as she processed the news. "Not the nicest of letters?" She let out a large intake of breath. "OK, yeah. Let me have it."

I slowly began to read out the letter and when I'd finished, Olivia was still silent.

"Are you OK?"

"She's just a bitch, isn't she? To be honest I don't think I expected anything else from her. There was no need to put in half of what she said. And I don't think we got anything of value from that, did we? Why didn't she answer whether they got married? They can't have been that happy if he didn't even want to marry her! I think she's full of shit." She spat the words angrily, her voice trembling with emotion. I felt completely responsible.

"Liv – I'm so sorry – this is all because of me. I shouldn't have raked up the past and I'm sorry that I got our hopes up for nothing."

"It's not your fault – it's *her*. She hasn't changed a bit, has she? She's still trying to be nasty and trying to hurt us. Why is she so bitter about everything?"

"I don't know. I'd have thought she would have calmed down after all these years. Maybe they weren't as happy as we thought they were?" I paused as I suddenly remembered the other part of the package. "She has sent some pictures. Let me send them to you."

"OK – look I'm going to have to go because I've got to put Louise to bed."

"Do you want to see a copy of the letter too?"

"Yes." She said after a short hesitation. "I'd like to show it to Danny and see what he thinks."

I felt like she was rushing me off the phone and I didn't blame her. I sat in my dining room and took pictures of the photocopies and the letter itself and sent them over to Olivia via Whatsapp. It took about half an hour before I'd received a reply:

```
OMG that's actually made me well up.  You
look so much like him.

                              Are you ok?
Yes I'm OK.
The younger ones are exactly how I
remember him
I can see us both in him.  I'm going to
read the letter when Louise's asleep.
```

I read Siobhan's letter a few more times. The reason he never wanted to see us again - the fact that he gave us up and cut all ties - was because we'd gone into the appointment room without him. I couldn't believe anyone would be so furious over something so trivial. It just felt incredibly petulant and there had to be more to it than that. I'd just remembered that he was late to the meeting because the welfare officer kept going out to check whether he'd arrived or not. Such a snap decision that he must have come to regret if it was made in that way. And I wondered what he'd found out about his marriage to Mum to make him doubt everything about it from day one. I recalled my mum's words the other week when she said Dad was still in love with her and how Siobhan knew it, which caused her to feel threatened. It was something that I actually remembered as a child, the fact that Dad wanted to get back with Mum. Siobhan described how they fell head over heels in love with each other the moment they met, *but they never got married*, which therefore didn't ring completely true. But then, they were together for over 35 years. I wondered how genuine Siobhan's letter had been; maybe it should all be taken with a pinch of salt? Was she overcompensating for what it was really like?

I began to calm down a little and looked at the pictures again, his confident, self-assured smile mocking me. What was going through his mind? Would his account of what happened match with Siobhan's? I took a deep breath before reading the letter again. One other thing that struck me was his illness – he had Motor Neurone Disease for twelve years, which was a ridiculously long time to suffer from that disease from the limited research I'd done. But if he'd had mild symptoms all the way to the end, maybe he didn't suffer. I guess he may have had some good medication to keep him going and lessen the effects. At least that was a good thing. But one thing that felt a little uncomfortable was the fact that my nan and Aunt both died from pancreatic cancer. Could there be a hereditary link here too? Another thing for my list when I see my GP.

The part about Uncle Harry was interesting. I wondered what his perspective would be on all of this. From the touching depiction of how Amanda raised his children, it sounded as though she in particular, might have been close to Siobhan, although there had clearly been no contact since Dad died. I sighed at the suggestion to contact Amanda and to pass on the copy of the letter to Harry; Siobhan must know that I had no way of getting in contact with them.

<u>Wednesday 13th November 2019</u>

I exchanged a few messages with Olivia later that night and throughout the following morning, and then we spoke briefly during my lunch break. Thankfully, she'd been able to talk things through with Daniel. She explained that she got upset when she saw the photos because Dad had looked so kind and just how we remembered him and it brought home how she couldn't understand why he gave us up; I wasn't sure we'd ever really find out. But although she was still a little emotional, at least Olivia appeared to be ok for now; she actually seemed to have taken it a lot better than I did and this surprised me somewhat. I had expected her to have a complete meltdown; in the past she had blown up over much smaller things. I wondered if she'd made her peace with it easier than I had when we were children? She'd had Mum and they'd had their girly chats and bonded on a female level, but I'd never had Dad, or any other male role model growing up. I never had father and son time, never had the opportunity to go down the pub for a beer with him or receive any fatherly advice from him. I'd always internalised things and tried to deal with my issues, finding some kind of resolution before I then told my mum about them. This had probably led to some of the mental health problems I'd experienced throughout my life, but it undoubtedly made me the independent man I am today.

It had been a long day with Siobhan's letter still weighing heavily. I still felt angry and let down but was able to channel my energy productively. I'd had a meeting with my boss earlier and I'd gone through everything on my plan that was still outstanding to complete. A lot of progress had been made and he seemed pleased with what had been done; however, this meant that my contract would not then be renewed beyond its expiry on 20th December. To be honest I felt that this was fair and was happy to be leaving on good terms. I wasn't entirely sure what the future held as new legislation being introduced from April next year would make it difficult for companies to employ freelance contactors, but it was something I didn't want to worry about today. It would be nice to have Christmas off and have a bit of a break from work and commuting. I had enough money in my company to see me through for about a year so there was no urgency to find work, and last year I decided to spend a few weeks in Australia, via Hong Kong and Singapore which was an amazing experience, so I wondered about doing something similar this coming January.

That evening, I was round Jane's and she read Siobhan's letter with interest.

"Well, it's the Siobhan show, isn't it?" She said shaking her head. "She could have been a little kinder in how she worded things."

I nodded in agreement. "Do you think she *was* trying to upset me? I don't get it. It's not how any normal person would react is it? And she seemed friendly enough with her first letter."

"Well, maybe she's not 'normal'". I looked at Jane curiously, wondering where she was going with this. "She's clearly not happy and not in a great place. You said yourself that the house didn't look as if it had been taken care of and I wonder if she's struggling to come to terms with the death of her partner who she was clearly deeply in love with. I wonder if she's struggling with depression, or some kind of mental illness?"

It suddenly made sense and it made me think back to the dark days I'd experienced when I'd had depression. It was the worst time of my life. It made me think irrationally and I was paranoid, thinking people were out to get me when looking back, they clearly weren't. I was lucky to have made it through; maybe Siobhan wasn't out the other side yet.

"The other theory I have is whether she took offence at your question asking whether they ever got married and had children... Was there anything else she missed out, or was that the only one she didn't answer?"

"You're right," I said slowly.

"It's probably one of the easier questions to answer in all honesty, but the implications are a little more far reaching."

"It might be why she went so over the top about how in love they were?" I sighed as the pennies began to drop.

"Yes, quite possibly. That makes a bit more sense now. So, do you think they weren't as happy as she claims?"

"I don't know. It's possible."

"I guess a lot of couples don't get married for so many reasons but bearing in mind he had a terminal illness and the house was in his sole name, it does seem odd. They could easily have got married in a registry office if they didn't want a big ceremony."

I nodded. "It's really making me wonder about the Will too – whether there is one or not. Even if he thumb-printed something on his death bed, anything could have been done as a last resort so that she would be taken care of."

"It might be that there is a Will but it's not favourable to Siobhan. Supposing they did have children and he left everything to them?"

I'd gone through this in my head so many times. "I don't know. None of it really adds up."

Jane wavered before the next question. "Has this changed your mind about what you want to do with the house?"

Admittedly it had crossed my mind. "The way I see it is that it's now a matter of principle. If there is a Will leaving everything to her, then fine – we'll walk away. If not, we're entitled to what we're entitled to and it should come to us." I hesitated. "The thing is, we may not have the option of letting her stay in the house; I guess inheritance tax will be payable and we don't have that amount of cash – so the house will have to be sold in order to pay it."

"I didn't think of that." Jane contemplated this issue. "This didn't affect me at all because I was married to James and there is a spousal exclusion, or something like that if you're married, which I guess they weren't." Jane screwed up her face. "Well, I think she's in for a bumpy ride! When are you thinking of starting things?"

"It's going to have to be after Christmas – I really don't want to do anything yet and I need to talk it through with Olivia first."

"Let me give you the name of the solicitor that helped me with James' Will. She was so helpful; professional but compassionate at the same time. Really guided me through everything."

"Thanks Jane, that would be brilliant!"

"Cool, I'll dig out her contact details for you. Her name is Jessica."

"The other thing is that I'm thinking of telling my mum all of this now. It just feels like it's getting a bit too big to keep from her. Especially the bit with the house, and if it turns out there will be more contact with Siobhan, I'd rather just come clean now before it all begins to spiral."

"What do you think her reaction will be?"

"I don't know. It could go either way – Olivia was actually ok with it in the end, but my mum does seem to make everything all about her, so who knows? There's only one way to find out!"

"She's calling my marriage a *sham?* What a nasty horrible bitch! Who does she think she is? *She's calling my marriage a sham?*"

"Those aren't exactly the words she used, Mum…"

"Oh, but that's what she's saying though isn't it? She doesn't know what she's talking about! I can't believe that *she* says that *my* marriage was a *sham!*"

This wasn't going brilliantly. I expected some kind of reaction when she read the letter, but Mum was incandescent. I'd popped round for lunch, as I did from time to time and it was actually her who brought up the subject of Dad and how I was feeling after the recent discovery. This was good – I'd planned to tell her anyway and she was open to talking about it, so it gave me a great opportunity to break the news. I'd let Olivia know that I was going to tell Mum, which she thought was the right thing to do, but was worried about her reaction. I also felt anxious at the thought of telling her, but reassured Olivia that it was better that she knew now than for us to *have* to tell her when it got too big.

I began by telling Mum that I did have some more questions and had done a bit more digging, finding out about the house still being in his name and the fact that there didn't appear to be a Will and the implications of this. At that point, it was as if Christmas had come early – a wide smile stretched across Mum's face as she processed this.

"So, what are you going to do? Are you going to kick her out? Oh, isn't it funny – what goes around comes around! She'll be sorry she ever messed with us!"

"Mum, I think it really comes down to principle, so if he did leave a Will, then we'll have to respect Dad's wishes, but otherwise who knows? I need to speak to a solicitor about it."

"So, you're serious about kicking her out then?"

"Look, I just need to understand where we stand before any decisions are made. But I don't want to do anything before Christmas – I don't want to rush into this and regret anything!"

I then started telling her about the letter I'd written to Siobhan, without including the fact that Olivia already knew. Mum was initially surprised about but accepted it relatively quickly, saying: "Well, I just wish you'd told me before! I bet she didn't reply though, did she?"

I pulled out the letter from Siobhan and handed it over to Mum, and that's when all hell broke loose. She read Siobhan's letter, eyes wide, gasping, tutting and puffing as she went; I could imagine the parts she was taking offence to. But it was really the sentence about how Dad began to doubt the marriage from day-one that Mum really lost it and had to stop reading to vent her anger.

"What a poisonous thing to say! I bet she knew you'd be showing this to me. She's still threatened by me – after all these years! Even after he's dead and buried! She's *still* threatened by me!"

"I do think she's still a bit bitter, but she might be suffering from depression, or something..."

"Depression? I'll give her *depression*! She doesn't know the meaning of the word! Did you know she never had any hardship whatsoever! She's never worked a day in her life! She was a kept woman. The rest of us had to scrimp and save and go without, just to put food on the table!"

"Mum, honestly. I'm not making excuses for her. And I didn't show this to you to upset you. I just didn't want to keep it from you anymore."

Mum continued to read, her lips pursed and head shaking throughout, still a few tuts and puffs, but quieter and a little calmer this time. Eventually, she finished.

"What a load of old rubbish. Not a word of truth in *any* of that. I don't even know why she even wrote back to you!" She paused for the briefest of moments. "No - I'll tell you why – to rub it in that she had everything, and you had nothing! Such a nasty, nasty piece of work!"

She held out the letter back to me, screwing up her mouth as if it smelled particularly bad.

"Well, now you know everything," I said, a little relieved that the initial explosion was relatively short-lived.

Mum got up and wandered into the kitchen to finish preparing lunch. I stayed in the living room, allowing her some space to process and to calm down a little more. Within 20 minutes or so, Mum emerged with two plates of roast chicken and veg. It smelled incredible and we both sat down to enjoy it. She smiled as we tucked in and she certainly seemed cooler than before, although her silence spoke volumes.

"Are you ok?"

"Look. I'm fine. I'm not going to let... *her* upset my Sunday with her ridiculous lies and half-truths. It's fine. *I'm fine.*"

I hesitated before my next question, not wanting to reignite her anger. "Mum, what did dad find out that made him doubt your marriage? I really don't want to upset you again – I just want to understand."

Mum narrowed her eyes and sighed deeply as she cast her mind back. "Look, you know I had an affair..."

"Yes... Was there more to it than that?"

"No! This is what she does! She twists things and manipulated your dad so that he thought there was more to it than there was. I mean, the person she's describing in her...

letter, isn't the man I remember. She's describing someone who was very forthright and decisive and he was none of those things. He was a kind man, happy to go with the flow, but a little weak. That's the main reason I left him because I needed an equal partner, someone I respected a bit more.

"It started maybe a couple of years before we split up. I was just feeling a bit lonely. I still loved your dad but I needed a little excitement. I didn't want to leave him, not at that point anyway but there was this man at badminton that I used to see every week while your dad was at work, and he was strong and respected and made me feel *safe* when I was around him. And this was something that I didn't have with your dad. Anyway, as the cliché goes, one thing led to another and we ended up having an affair which was wonderful while it lasted – but he was married too, and he broke it off very quickly. But I ended up telling your dad and he was so kind and understanding about it. He said he knew something was up and actually felt relieved that I'd told him and that I wasn't going to leave him. That kind of gave us a second wind – he became a bit more attentive and things began to improve between us, but ultimately, we were different people and I wanted something different – I *needed* something more. Anyway, things came to a head – I don't know if you remember but we had some awful rows...?"

"Mum, I remember," I said, a little incredulous that Mum thought I might have forgotten the endless screaming, shouting and slamming of doors as a child.

"Well, anyway, things came to a head and that's when we split up and he moved out. Now – it was a good few months afterwards that I met Alf, and then your dad was saying to me that he had met Siobhan and was kind of asking for my blessing to take her out, which I was all for obviously – I thought it would keep him happy and let us get on with our new lives. But very soon, Siobhan had convinced him all sorts of things had happened and that Alf was the man I'd carried on with while we were still married – and that I'd never loved your dad – but that wasn't the case at all. It was all lies. So that's why I feel so angry with her for still carrying this on!" Her voice began to rise as she recalled Siobhan and the apparent manipulation. I wasn't sure whether Siobhan had deliberately gone out of her way to cause trouble, or whether she genuinely believed what she had said. And then I thought of the letter and realised that she just seemed to be a nasty person. How was Dad ever happy with her? Even if he loved her deeply, surely her bitterness would wear thin and become tiresome and petty after a while?

Another thing crossed my mind. "Mum, what documents do you think Siobhan would have that would have had my date of birth and full name on them? Dad didn't keep our birth certificates, did he?"

"No! I have all of those. I even have his dad's death certificate. He never wanted to deal with any kind of administration." Mum paused again. "That's what makes it so unusual about the house being in his name only – he always wanted everything in joint names because he didn't want to deal with the mortgage or bills or anything like that. He can't've been that happy with her, could he? Why wouldn't he put everything in her name just to make it easier for her after he died?"

"Mum, what other documents could Siobhan have that would have that information on it?" I pressed on, trying to get back to the point I was trying to make.

Mum shook her head, blank expression on her face. "I've no idea. I can't think of anything official... Unless he just kept a record of that information? I don't know."

"Mum – would a *Will* have that kind of information on it?"

Mum's face lit up again. "You know what – you might be on to something! That's why she's such a bitch to you! She thinks you're going to take everything away from her!" She paused as another thought came to her. "How on earth are you ever going to tell Olivia about any of this? I'm sure she'll love the news about the house – but you can't tell her about the letter. It'll destroy her!"

Olivia listened to my account with what felt like relief and bemusement.

"I can't believe she doesn't want me to know!"

"It's not that – she's just trying to protect you. Just call her and tell her you know and then that will be that. And from now on, anything – *anything at all* – that I find out I'll make sure that you both know."

"So, what are you going to find out next?"

"Who knows? I never expected half of this to be honest. I just wish I could find Uncle Harry and get his account of what happened."

It was a rainy afternoon and I'd finished my last meeting of the day. I was sitting at my desk, not really wanting to get involved in anything else but it was only 3pm. After I wandered to the kitchen to make a coffee, I sat back down at my desk and started a Google search for my Uncle Harry.

The search initially took me to 192 Online, which appeared to be the old Directory Enquiries service that you used to dial 192 to find out someone's phone number or address. I'd typed in Harry's name and provided the address as "Hackney" and no results came up. After looking on my phone to find his middle initial from the *Ancestry* search I'd done a few years ago, and trying another couple of variations, I changed the address to just show "London". My heart stopped as two results came up.

One was for an address in Homerton, which was a district in Hackney. Could this be him? I clicked on the entry, which then pulled up more information than I was expecting. It seemed like 192 Online pulled through any publicly available information to the site, so information from the electoral register also appeared. It showed that Harry and Amanda Walters lived at the address, and that Lee, Darren and Richard Walters had previously lived there but had now moved out. His three sons? This had to be him! I took a deep breath as I processed this information. I had found my Uncle Harry after 35 years of not seeing him. Harry, my dad's younger brother, who was always kind and interested and took time to talk to us – and seemed to care about us. *But that was then.* What reception would I get if I contacted him? Would he want to hear from me? What would Dad have told him? Surely Harry would be sensible enough to make his own mind up.

Out of curiosity, I typed in Siobhan O'Reilly, Canvey Island and immediately up came Siobhan's address. When I clicked on it, it showed to my amazement that Siobhan no longer lived at the address – she appeared to have left in 2016 – *when Dad died*. But my dad in all accounts still showed to be living there. What was going on? Siobhan surely was still living at the address. And Dad was clearly not! Either there had been some kind of administrative error, or Siobhan had lied to the authorities to falsify information about Dad dying. Was she masquerading as my dad? How fucked up was that? So, she must have kept everything in his name and if they had a joint bank account, she was still able to access everything – his pension, his government benefits. *Everything.* This was pretty significant fraud. And all because there probably wasn't a Will and nothing had been transferred to her name. Would we ever really find out what really happened?

The other thing that struck me was how easy it was to find out this information. All those years of wondering where Dad was, the Instagram, Facebook and Twitter searches, and a two-minute internet search could have found him while he was still alive.

<u>**Thursday 21st November 2019**</u>

I slept on this information, to decide whether to contact Harry or not and overwhelmingly came to the conclusion, multiple times, that yes, I should. When I arrived at work in the morning, after my 9am meeting, I quickly typed up a letter and printed it off, reading it a final time before sealing in in an envelope. I decided to keep as neutral as I could with regards to Siobhan so as not to cause any offence, depending on their relationship with her:

Dear Harry

I'm Colin, James's son. I hope you don't mind me contacting you – I recently found out that James passed away in 2016, which left me wanting to find out more about his life since I last saw him.

I did write to Siobhan having found their address on James's death certificate, but her response didn't provide much insight and I still have a few questions. Please can I assure you that the last thing I want to do is stir up the past and cause any trouble or bad feeling. I just want to find out a bit more about my dad's life since the time I saw him last.

With that in mind, would you consider meeting up for a drink? If so, please let me know what would work best for you. It would also be wonderful to see you again after all this time.

Very best wishes,

Colin

I posted it during my lunch hour, feeling more apprehensive than I had done before. I prayed that I'd get a positive response this time.

<u>Sunday 24th November 2019</u>

The last few days had been a whirlwind. After I'd sent the letter to Harry on Thursday, to my surprise, I'd received an email from him on Friday afternoon. It was a nice, friendly email and it came though while I was at work and was sent as a Word attachment:

Dear Colin

It was so nice to hear from you after so many years; I have thought about you and Olivia from time to time.

Colin, Siobhan holds her cards so close to her chest that there isn't much I can tell you, but I'm willing to fill in any gaps I can, and it would certainly be nice to see you after all these years. I'm not so keen to drink these days, but you'd be welcome to come to my home and we can discuss your dad as much as we are able.

You have my address, but if you prefer, we can email or phone. Whichever way, feel free to contact me again and we can arrange things.

Look forward to seeing you.

Harry

P.S. I've just seen your email address. I'll contact you.

It was so warm and such a contrast to Siobhan's letter it actually brought tears to my eyes, much to the shock of Temi, my work colleague sitting opposite me. She asked if I was ok and then dragged me into a room when she saw the emotion beginning to leak out of me. I hadn't told anyone at work what had been going on and I really didn't want to start now. Temi was lovely and we had grown pretty close over the past year or so I'd been working with her, so I just told her I'd found my Uncle who I hadn't seen since I was a child and I never thought I'd see him again (which was true). She sat with me for about 10 minutes while I was able to compose myself, which I was grateful for.

I reread Harry's letter again and wondered what was behind the comment about Siobhan keeping her cards close to her chest. It didn't sound like they were on the best of terms, but surely, he'd be able to tell me a bit more information about Dad and fill in some of the gaps in Siobhan's account. When I got home, I'd texted Harry (he'd included a mobile number in his letter):

> Hi Harry, it's Colin. Thanks so much for your email. Are you free now for me to give you a quick call?

It was over an hour before he came back:

> You can call now if you like, Colin

And so with a pounding heart I called my uncle.

Harry's voice was calm, gentle and familiar. His subtle East End accent was comforting and friendly, and I pictured him as I remembered him; slim, dark curly hair, stubbly beard and glasses. Inevitably he sounded older, and a little overwhelmed at speaking to me. The conversation flowed although I got the impression he was a little suspicious of my true motives; however I explained how I'd found out Dad had died and the letter I'd received from Siobhan. I played it safe and was tactful, just saying that it didn't provide much more information. Harry explained he hadn't seen Dad for a few years before he died, although still spoke warmly of him. He was interested in the interaction I'd had with Siobhan, so I talked in a bit more detail about the letters that had been exchanged between us. I kept to the facts and tried not to let on how hurt I'd been at her response. Harry listened and paused after I'd finished.

"Oh, what are we going to do about your Dad," he said, almost as if he didn't know what else to say.

"Would it be OK for me to come round to see you? I'd really like to know a little more about Dad's life and what happened, and it would be amazing to see you again in the flesh. It must've been 35 years!"

"Has it really? Goodness me!"

"I'm free on Sunday if that works for you?"

"Well, yes, of course.... It'll have to be in the afternoon...?" He sounded hesitant but even so, I persisted.

"How about 2.30?"

"Yes, yes. It would be wonderful to see you too. I can't believe it's been that long!" He sounded calmer, more accepting of the arrangement now. And then we said our goodbyes.

I had a quick call each with Mum and Olivia to let them both know I'd found Harry and that I was going to see him and Amanda on Sunday. Mum sounded excited and even asked if she could come too, but I said that I didn't want to overwhelm him with all of us turning up, and depending how things went, she could maybe come along next time. Olivia was equally excited and said how wonderful it would be for Louise to meet some more of the extended family – the only family on her side were me and Mum so to meet her Great Uncle would be lovely.

On Sunday I made sure I was dressed well and was clean shaven. I took the photocopied letter from Siobhan and the additional copies of the pictures of Dad that she'd sent me; after all, she had given me copies to pass on to Harry. I also decided to take a recent family photo that I had of me, Mum, Olivia, Louise and Daniel, just so he could see us all, and maybe slowly introduce the idea of him meeting everyone else at some point in the future. My mind was spinning as I drove down the A12 on the way to Hackney; this had all happened so fast and I wasn't really able to fully take it all in. The journey would take just under an hour, so I left at around 1.25 in case of traffic. It was slightly overcast but otherwise the conditions were fine. Presently, I saw the familiar sights of the Olympic Park in Stratford, and then within a couple of minutes, the railings of Victoria Park, where Dad used to take us when we came round to visit him at his mum's, my nan. Harry lived in Brookfield Road, the road behind where Nan used to live, both branching off Victoria Park Road. I turned into Brookfield Road at around 2.25 – right on time and pulled up a few doors away from Harry's house. I took a deep breath before I got out of my car.

Brookfield Road was a typical Hackney street; lined with Victorian town houses, some better maintained than others, but all striking and impressive, nonetheless. The outside of Harry's house was neat and well maintained with a paved garden and a potted conifer tree to the left of the front door. As I opened the gate to Harry's house and rang the bell my heart was beating slightly faster than before. Within a couple of minutes, the door was opened by an elderly lady in a pale blue flowing dress and white cardigan. The smell of fabric conditioner poured out of the door. She beamed when she saw me.

"You must be Colin! Come on in!"

"Thank you! You must be Amanda? Lovely to meet you."

As I came inside an elderly man was slowly coming down the stairs. Initially I didn't recognise him, but this was Harry. He had put on a lot of weight over the past 35 years, had short cropped grey hair and was clean shaven. He wasn't wearing glasses, so must have had laser eye surgery, or maybe he was wearing contact lenses. He smiled broadly as he saw me.

"Right on time – just like your dad!" he exclaimed as he shook my hand vigorously. Noticing my puzzled expression, he added, "Your dad was always so punctual – to the minute! I said to Amanda – 'I wonder whether we'll be able to set our watches to Colin too!' It's good to see you again, Colin."

I hated being late for anything and was surprised that this was a family trait that I'd appeared to have inherited. I became excited to find out if there were other traits that we shared.

After I took my coat off, Harry and Amanda ushered me along the hallway to the kitchen and I took a seat at a small dining table. I was offered a coffee and a chocolate éclair and immediately felt welcome and comfortable in their company. Their house had the typical layout of any house built during the Victorian period – kitchen at the back; living and dining room to the front; stairs to the side – it felt cosy and traditional. It didn't look as if it had been decorated for a number of years, although it was tidy and well maintained.

I gave him the photo I'd brought of Olivia, Louise, Daniel, my mum and me. "This is all of us," I said, pointing out everyone in the picture.

"Oh My!   Your mum's changed, hasn't she?" exclaimed Harry as he examined the photo carefully.

'Haven't we all!' I thought as I watched him carefully. "Olivia was so keen to meet you and introduce Louise to you, but instead of piling everyone round I thought I'd give you a photo to begin with."

"How lovely!" said Amanda as Harry passed the photo to her. "You and your sister look a lot like your dad." She looked at me and spoke carefully, her voice tinged with an air of melancholy, not entirely sure what my reaction would be.

"Well, yes. I guess I could see the resemblance… Siobhan included some pictures of Dad with the letter she sent." I dug those out and passed them to Harry.

"My, my, my. There he is, the old rascal himself." Harry was lost momentarily gazing at the pictures of his brother. "Can I take copies of these?"

"They're yours – Siobhan sent them to me to pass on to you. I have my own copies."

Harry's face lit up. "I don't have any pictures of your dad. How wonderful. Thank you for bringing them over!"

I thought it strange that Harry didn't have any pictures of Dad at all. Maybe he wasn't the sentimental type.

When I finished my chocolate éclair, Amanda suggested we move into the living room, where she said it would be more comfortable. They led the way back down the hall and turned right into the living room. I took a seat in a large soft armchair near the bay window that I sunk into and had to sit up not to slouch. Harry sat in a sturdier armchair opposite me and Amanda was on the sofa facing the bay window.

"Thanks for agreeing to see me," I started, looking at both of them.

"It's wonderful to have you!" said Amanda. "I was saying to Harry, how funny it was that you decided to contact us now. It was not even two weeks ago that we were talking about you and your sister!" She smiled, shaking her head in disbelief.

"Really? How come?"

"Well, we hadn't heard from Siobhan in such a long time, and we wondered whether she was still alive – and if not – well, that house – it's your inheritance!"

"Oh, goodness." I didn't know what else to say. I didn't want to explain everything I'd found out – not just yet anyway, but what a bizarre coincidence that while I was finding out the possibility of the house legally belonging to us, Harry and Amanda – who I hadn't been in contact with for 35 years – were thinking the same thing. "How strange!" I looked at Harry who was studying me with interest. I wondered if he'd suspected what I'd been up to over the past couple of weeks. I remembered Siobhan's letter and passed it over to Harry. "This was the letter that Siobhan sent with the photos."

Harry read it quickly, without reaction, handing it to Amanda within a couple of minutes.

"Oh Harry, what does it say?" said Amanda.

"Not very much." Harry sighed dismissively.

Amanda took more time reading the letter, looking thoughtful as she did.

"Harry, do you mind me asking you what happened with Dad, after he…. Well, since we last saw him?"

"Yes, yes, of course." He shifted in his chair to make himself more comfortable. "Your dad was always very easily influenced. He used to follow our cousin Pete around and do whatever Pete said. He'd go to the wrestling on a Friday night, go to the pub on a Thursday; whatever Pete said was the law. And then Siobhan came along. Your dad changed when Siobhan came on the scene, almost overnight. It must have been around the time that he last saw you, he moved out of your nan's house and into Siobhan's house with her parents. Now, they only lived a stone's throw from each other."

"I remember – Siobhan and her parents lived across the road, didn't they?"

"Yes, that's right – they lived opposite Mum's house – your grandmother's house. Well, when your dad moved in with Siobhan, he hardly ever came back to see us. Only Christmases, birthdays, and maybe the other odd occasion, but it was very few and far between. It really upset your nan. Even when she was dying from cancer, he didn't visit her in hospital that often and I don't think she ever got over it." Harry bowed his head.

My nan was a typical East End lady; the door was always open and there was always room for another person to pull up a chair at the dining table. I remember the times when we were there, it was always chaos with people dropping in, but it was chaos that she revelled in. And she loved being the centre of it all and thoroughly enjoyed her role as the matriarch. I can imagine she was incredibly hurt when Dad saw her so infrequently. And to not see her when she was dying from cancer was awful.

"Anyway, they moved into the house in Canvey. It was a big house – it had an annex where Siobhan's parents lived with them, but contact became even more infrequent when they moved there; we'd still see them for the odd Christmas and other family events, like weddings and funerals and that was it, wasn't it, Amanda?"

"Well, we did go round there once, didn't we?" Amanda said. "Shortly after they moved to Canvey, they invited us round, with the kids, and Deb and Terry – you know, your aunt and her husband. It was kind of a housewarming dinner party. She put on a lovely spread, and I did think that as vegetarians, she was kind to serve up chicken for the children."

"They were *vegetarians*? Dad too?" Dad was never a vegetarian while I knew him! He didn't think a meal was complete without meat.

"Yes – I don't know when he stopped eating meat, but yes he was a vegetarian."

"And Siobhan's parents lived with them too?"

"Yes – they both died quite a few years back now, but yes – one of the reasons they bought the house was because it was able to accommodate her parents, whilst still giving them some space of their own.

"Anyway," continued Harry, "That was up until Steve's wedding. Steve is Pete's son. Your dad and Siobhan were invited to the wedding and they said they were going to be there – your dad wouldn't have missed it for the world – but they didn't turn up, and that was very out of character – if your dad said he'd be somewhere, he'd always be there. Or he'd call to say that he was running late or if something else had happened meaning he couldn't make it, but to just not turn up, and to *Steve's* wedding as well, it was very odd. We were quite worried, and everyone was asking after him."

"Your dad and Steve were so close. He loved Steve, *like a son*." Amanda stopped abruptly and stared at me as she said this, realising the impact of what she'd said. I tried not to react, but it hit me like a bolt. He loved Steve like a son, but didn't love me... his *actual* son.

There was the briefest of awkward silences and then Harry continued. "After the wedding, I tried ringing your dad but there was no answer, and then I wrote to him and he didn't reply. You can imagine, we were all getting really worried now, so your cousin, Matthew, you know – Deb's boy? He, Pete and I decided to go round their house and see what was going on. We saw your dad's car parked outside when we arrived, and I knocked on the door, but no-one answered. Matthew saw Siobhan at the window too. She saw us and Matthew looked directly in her eyes, but she still didn't answer the door. We stayed there, knocking, thinking that as she'd seen us – and she'd seen that we'd seen *her*, she'd definitely open the door, but she didn't. None of us could believe it! We wondered what on earth had happened.

"Well, after that, we were going to call the police, weren't we Amanda? That's right – Matthew was all for calling the police and knocking the door down. We suspected foul play, you see; quite understandably given the circumstances."

"Yes, yes, but you then received the letter, didn't you?"

"Oh, that's right. I received a reply to the letter I'd written to your dad. It was very blunt, just saying something along the lines of, 'I'm fine, there's no need to contact me.' Now, again this was out of character and it didn't look like your dad's writing. He always had very neat writing, and this was all over the place. We actually wondered whether Siobhan had written the letter, but now, seeing the letter she'd written to you, her writing was nothing like what we received." Amanda nodded in agreement. "So, after that, we were still going to call the police..."

"But then Pete managed to speak to him."

"Yes, Pete was able to get hold of him over the phone and spoke to him. And your dad was very calm and very clear and said there was no need to get in touch with him again. Obviously, we were all terribly upset, but Pete said that he'd been very definite, and we couldn't force him to see us or stay in touch if he really didn't want to. And that was the last any of us saw or heard from him."

I was almost numb; it sounded like something out of a murder mystery. I couldn't believe what I'd just heard, and a chill ran through me, making me visibly shudder. "Can you remember when this was?"

Harry screwed up his face and looked at the ceiling. "It must have been about... 15 years ago?" Amanda nodded in support. "Yes – it's got to be about 15 years ago. Something like that."

"Wasn't that the time he got Motor Neurone Disease? Siobhan said he was diagnosed in 2004."

Harry held his hand out to Amanda for Siobhan's letter and she duly passed it back to him. He scanned it again.

"My boy, you're right. The thing is, we had no idea he had Motor Neurone Disease until after he died."

"Really? When did you find out?"

"Well, after your dad's phone call with Pete, no-one heard from him or Siobhan again. Until that is, she called me out of the blue to tell me he'd died the day before and that he had Motor Neurone Disease. She said that she hadn't told us before because *he* didn't want any of us to know. He didn't want his *family* to know he had a terminal illness." Harry sighed and looked down. "That was the first that we knew he'd been ill."

"Thinking of it now though, Harry, do you remember we were at another wedding?" said Amanda thoughtfully. "I can't remember for the life of me whose it was, but it was maybe 6 months or so before Steve's? And James and Siobhan were there? We saw Siobhan cutting up your dad's food for him, because he was clearly struggling with a knife and fork, but we just thought it was arthritis."

"Yes, yes, I do remember that. That was also odd because that evening, quite early on they just disappeared without saying goodbye to anyone, and we were looking all over for them. I suppose he could have been suffering back then too."

This was quite different to Siobhan's account. I remember her letter clearly stated that his symptoms were very mild up to when he died. Why would she even lie about that?

"But then there was a long wait for the death certificate, wasn't there Harry?" Amanda said, "I remember thinking this was odd because he had a terminal illness and, from my experience, provided that you're seen by a medical professional within 7 days of dying from a terminal illness, a death certificate can just be issued without any post-mortem or anything."

"Amanda was a Macmillan nurse, so she knows all about those kinds of procedures," Harry added, with a sad smile at his wife.

"We were due to go on holiday, weren't we, Harry? And we were waiting for the funeral to be arranged to know whether we could go or not."

"That's right. I remember chasing Siobhan up and telling her that we were going away for a week, so please arrange the funeral outside of that week because we really wanted to attend. But finally, after three weeks of waiting for the death certificate to arrive, she chose to arrange the funeral slap bang in the middle of the week were we due to go away. It was a trip to Norway and she only gave us a days' notice."

"We'd already packed and were about to leave!"

"And so, we ended up missing his funeral. That was the last we ever heard from her."

We sat silently for a few moments and I contemplated everything I'd just been told. Supposing it was true that Dad didn't want anyone to know about his illness, Siobhan was just carrying out his wishes and despite how hurtful it would be to his family, it was him that supposedly wrote the letter, and Pete definitely spoke to him on the phone. But for Siobhan to arrange the funeral during a week when she knew that Harry, his brother, couldn't attend was heartless. I was shocked again at the nastiness of Siobhan's actions.

"That's awful." I said quietly, breaking the silence. Harry nodded. "You were so close, though. I remember when I was little, you'd always be laughing and joking together."

"Yes, that's right. We always had banter and were the best of friends. But your dad was not just easily influenced, he needed to be told what to do, he need to be dominated I suppose. There was one time, I can't remember what it was, but he asked Siobhan whether or not to put something in the boot of the car! He needed *that level of direction*!" Harry spoke with frustration, yet resignation. It was clear he was still hurt by everything that had happened but seemed to have accepted that there was a sense of inevitability about it.

"I have to say, I expected a little more from her letter." I chose my words carefully, not wanting to overstep the mark. "I expected her to want to tell me about their time together – the hobbies they shared, the films they loved; the places they'd been, but there was really nothing in it that gave any information about *their life.*"

"Oh, they loved going up to the West End and your dad was a huge James Bond fan so they'd take a taxi to Leicester Square and they'd get all dressed up – your dad would wear a tuxedo – and they'd see the first showing of the new James Bond film!" Amanda was talking enthusiastically, smiling gently as she spoke. I thought back to the photos that

Siobhan sent, including the one of Dad in a tux. That must have been one of the times they were on their way to Leicester Square. It was a nice change of tone from the dark conversation we'd shared moments before.

"Your dad was such a practical joker too. He had a wicked sense of humour. Some of the things he'd come out with!" Harry smiled fondly as he recalled happier memories. "It will be lovely to see him again." He looked warmly at Amanda, then glanced at me and saw my bewildered expression. "Amanda and I believe that after we die, we are all reunited with the people we have loved. There are some pertinent passages in The Bible that have certainly given me comfort and continue to do so."

I smiled gently at him. I wasn't religious and didn't think that any of Dad's family were. Maybe it was after Harry's wife, Christine, had died that he was able to find peace through the church. Well good for him if he did.

"I really wish I'd found you sooner." I said, "It was so easy – I didn't realise how easy it would have been before I started the search."

"How *did* you find us?" said Harry inquisitively.

"You were on 192.Online – the twenty first century version of Directory Enquiries. It was really easy!"

"Oh, and your dad would have loved to have seen you again, before he died," said Amanda. I'm sure she meant well, but I couldn't help feeling that after everything I'd been told, that may not have been true.

"Well, who knows?" I said, gently, pausing before I asked the next question. "Harry, can I ask… What reason did Dad give for not wanting to see us anymore?"

Harry looked at me. "First of all, can you tell me what happened, as you remember it?"

I explained that when Siobhan came on the scene, visits to us became more sporadic, the rows about maintenance money and the meeting at the Welfare Office when he told us to our faces that he wasn't going to see us again. Harry listened intently to my account and then took a few moments as he picked up and reviewed Siobhan's letter again.

"That all ties in with Siobhan's account."

"Did Dad give a different story?"

"Your dad never wanted to talk about what happened with you and your sister. Of course, we asked what had happened. I knew that the divorce had been difficult, and it had got quite bitter, but that had nothing to do with the two of you." Harry sighed deeply. "When I really pressed him, he just said he had no choice... He told me he was threatened at knife point."

"*What?* Do you mean like... domestic violence?" Of all the things I was expecting to hear, I never expected to hear this.

Harry shrugged. "I don't know. Can you make any sense of that?"

"No. I'm absolutely gobsmacked!" I think Harry could see how shocked I was at this revelation.

"It's something that I could never understand, myself." Harry added. "I mean, whatever happens, you can never break the emotional bond of your children, regardless of the circumstances."

I nodded. "I can relate to that. I feel the same way about Louise, Olivia's daughter, and she's not even mine. I guess he never spoke about us, then?"

"Not to me, no. But I'm sure he must have thought about you both over the years. He wouldn't have been able not to." Harry paused. "So, what about you? Are you married? You don't have any children of your own, then?"

"No, I'm single. I... I haven't found the right one just yet."

Harry nodded, keeping his gaze fixed. I wasn't quite ready to come out to him, but I guessed that I probably wouldn't have to. He had a knowing look in his eyes.

"How's Abigail? We used to have so much fun with her when we were kids!" I said.

Harry hesitated and broke his gaze. "Did you? Oh, how funny." Amanda shifted in her seat a little. "I... err, I haven't seen Abi in quite some time, it must have been about 9 years now, I think. She's doing well, though. I see updates through Facebook and I see that she has two children now."

What was with this family? Was anyone still in touch with anyone at all? It seemed that everyone had been estranged at some point. I desperately wanted to know what had happened between them; what had caused them to not stay in touch and for Harry to find out she had children – the fact that he had *grandchildren* – through Facebook. Harry clearly didn't want to talk about it, and I wasn't going to probe any further and make him feel uncomfortable.

"Let me call Matthew," said Harry suddenly and reached for his mobile phone.

"Deb's son? My cousin?"

Harry nodded with a smile as he found Matthew's number and started the call. "Matthew? How the devil are you?... Splendid! I'm in very good health, thank you!... Oh, I don't know – it was your wedding the last time I saw you? It must have been!... Five years? That long?... My, my, time certainly flies, my boy!... Now, I'll give you a guess as to who is sitting in front of me, large as life!" There was silence as Matthew contemplated the conundrum presented to him.

"OK, I'll tell you – it's Colin! James's son? You remember…?" Harry was beaming as he looked at me during the conversation, enjoying the undoubtedly surprised reaction coming back from Matthew, another long-lost family member. "Do you want to have a word?... Oh, let me pass you over!"

Suddenly and feeling quite unprepared, Harry thrust his iPhone into my hand with Matthew on the other end asking how I was and congratulating me for getting in contact. Another whirlwind moment. We established that I was 9 and Matthew was 18 the last time we saw each other. I was now 44 and he was 53. He owned his own cleaning business and drove past our old house in Elm Park the other week. I explained the job I had and suddenly remembered that Dad had given Matthew his old motorbike, which Matthew fell off shortly afterwards, and broke his leg.

"Actually, my foot was severed, and they managed to save it and reattach it, no idea how they did, but they did. Funny what they don't tell you as a kid, eh?" My stomach lurched at the thought. Matthew was easy to talk to. He came across as a genuinely nice guy and the conversation flowed for a couple of minutes. "Listen, get Harry to give you my number and we'll meet up for a drink. Let's see if we can get something in before Christmas!"

"That would be great!" I was genuinely delighted to have reconnected with him.

Before I knew it, I was handing the phone back to Harry, who had a few final words with Matthew, wished him well and that was it. Harry fiddled on his phone and I received a text from Harry with Matthew's number on it. I saved it immediately.

As I said my goodbyes, I again remembered Olivia and Mum wanting to meet Harry, so I suggested that they come next time.

"Absolutely! *Please* bring the family next time," said Harry warmly. "It would be wonderful to see everyone again and to meet little Louise!"

"Yes – I'll make us all some lunch," added Amanda. "It would be so lovely to meet everyone!"

I left around 5.30. It was dark and beginning to rain. The windscreen wipers squealed as they flicked the drops away, as I found my way to the North Circular, and then more familiar territory on the M25. Despite the warmness of the welcome I had with Harry, and how lovely it had been to see him and meet Amanda, I felt a little numb with an underlying feeling of sadness and uneasiness at what they'd told me.

I needed to get my head around everything I'd found out. The story made me think of an old Kathy Bates film, where a man is kept prisoner in bed and Kathy Bates' character cares for him out of some obsessive love she had for him. It's a pretty intense film and the prisoner succumbs to horrendous injuries but eventually manages to escape. *No such escape for Dad*. I wondered how happy he'd actually been and whether he'd regretted meeting Siobhan, or whether he was as in love with her as she was with him and was happy and grateful for everything she did for him. The fact that he needed to be dominated lingered with me. It was Siobhan who called all the shots – despite her saying otherwise in her letter – but at what cost? To give up your children, cut ties with your family, including your dying mother – all because of the need to be dominated? Or did this come down to a weakness in my dad? It also made me think of the stories I'd heard of domestic abuse survivors who'd been beaten down so much they felt worthless, but eventually found the courage and strength to escape and find liberation again. I wondered, if with Dad and Siobhan, it was not necessarily abuse but a form of control that he was happy to sign up to, and even needed at some level. The fact that Siobhan played down his illness and said he was strong to the end, which conflicted with Harry's account a year or so prior to his diagnosis was also worrying. What if he got to the point where he was completely incapacitated, he was being fed through a tube and regretted everything that had brought him to this point in his life? There would have been no way out; he may not even have been able to communicate this, whether anyone would have been willing to listen. He'd have had regular check ins from GPs or hospital staff, but would they have had the power or the inclination to do anything about it? Would they have taken anything he said seriously if Siobhan had played down everything he'd said? It just sounded like such a lonely existence, and Dad was such a sociable man, I can't imagine him wanting to cut ties with his brother and Pete... And Steve. The thought of Steve made me even more sad. Had Dad found a replacement son? A replacement for me? Maybe he did miss me? He *must* have thought about us, even fleetingly for a few minutes? I thought, not for the first time, that had I'd been a better son, *maybe as good as Steve,* I'd have still been in his life and he wouldn't have given us up. I knew it sounded ridiculous to think that way as a grown man, when my dad abandoned us as children, but deep down I couldn't get away from that feeling. I pushed that thought to the back of my mind as another thought quickly replaced it.

The comment about being held at knifepoint. What could this have meant? Who could have done such a thing? I'm sure my mum wouldn't have had anything to do with it? Could Siobhan have? Could she have threatened him? Or maybe she threatened to hurt herself if he didn't cut ties with us? The confusion continued all the way home, and as seemed to be the case with all of this, the more I thought about what I'd found out, the more questions I seemed to have.

When I got in, I made myself a coffee and then called Mum.

"How'd you get on?" She sounded a little anxious.

"It was fine." I tried to sound calm and relaxed before I launched into everything. "They were lovely and welcoming, and I found out loads. They were very polite, but I don't think they like Siobhan."

"Did you tell them that she said my marriage was a sham?"

I sighed as I rolled my eyes. "*Mum*, I gave Harry a copy of Siobhan's letter, so he saw what she wrote."

"And did he say what a nasty piece of work she was?"

"Mum, come on! Like I said – they were very polite, but I don't think they were Siobhan's biggest fans. It's quite a story.

I relayed Harry's version of events from the widening gap between Dad and Siobhan, and the rest of the family, including with his mum when she was ill in hospital.

"Oh, that would have devasted her," said Mum quietly. "She was the head of the house in every sense and the force that held everyone together, and for him to drop her like he did, I can imagine she would have been heartbroken. Don't you see, now. None of what happened was personal to you if he did this – if *she* did this – to his mum."

Believe it or not, that hadn't actually occurred to me. I think I was so lost in the weeds of it all I hadn't considered the wider impact. I paused as I considered this for a couple of seconds, taking into account the rest of the story and it seemed to stack up. "I think you're right, Mum." I still felt a little numb but in a very twisted kind of way, it felt ever so slightly comforting.

I carried on telling Mum what happened, all the way up to the point where Harry and Amanda weren't able to go to the funeral.

"What an evil witch!" Mum exclaimed, her voice filled with emotion and anger. "Why would anyone do such a nasty, evil thing? Even when he died, she wanted him all to herself! She's awful! Such a nasty, nasty bitch!"

"I really don't understand it either," I said, trying to sound as calm as possible. "I also don't get why it took so long for the death certificate to be issued if he had a terminal illness. That doesn't make sense at all."

"I think she was just stalling. She didn't want anyone else to come to the funeral and she held off arranging any of it until she knew Harry was off on holiday and it was too late to do anything about it. She's so calculating! Such an evil woman!"

"Mum, are you ok?"

"Yes – I'm just shocked. There was I, well, all of us I suppose, thinking he'd gone off and had this wonderful life and all along he was being locked up and was probably as miserable as sin."

"Mum," I hesitated as I seemed to do so often these days, "There was something else Harry mentioned."

"Go on." Mum sounded like she had prepared herself for the worst.

"When I asked Harry if Dad had ever spoken about me and Olivia, and whether he gave a reason for not seeing us, Harry said that Dad had told him that he'd had no choice because... Because he'd been threatened at knife point."

"You *what?*"

"You've no idea where that came from, do you?"

"Look – I may have been many things, but I've never tried to stop your dad seeing you – and I'd never threaten him with a *knife!*"

"*Mum,* I'm not accusing you! I just wondered if you knew where it came from? If there was something that you knew that you didn't tell us at the time?"

"I've no idea. I've never heard that before – I swear to you! I've never heard of such a thing!"

"The thing I don't understand was why Harry just seemed to accept it. I mean, even if a good friend had said something like that to me, I wouldn't have settled for it. And I'm amazed that Harry allowed Dad to have accepted it so easily. I'd have rallied the family, got him to contact the police – he already knew Paul and could obviously pull some strings? It all seems like the reaction was, 'oh well, never mind, let's move on'. That doesn't add up at all. And generally, the more I've thought about it, the more I can't see how it would have happened – unless it was Siobhan with the knife, either threatening to hurt him or even herself."

"Maybe Harry knew at a deeper level that Siobhan had taken him over and it was her calling the shots with regards to you two. And he didn't know how to handle it. Not saying it was right, but I suppose he knew that decisions had been made and the damage had already been done and there was no coming back from it."

We went backwards and forwards on this, covering the same ground a few times, still coming to the same unanswered questions and not really getting anywhere. Then the other question that I had came forward in my mind. "Harry also said that Siobhan's parents lived in the house in Canvey with them – it had a separate annex and that's the reason they bought it – so to me, it makes no sense that the house is in his sole name. Surely, the parents would have sold the house in Hackney and the money from that would have been put down as a deposit for the Canvey house? The parents would have wanted some kind of security for themselves, as well as Siobhan, so for no provision to be made makes no sense at all."

"You're right – I can't see that any one of them being that lax about the whole thing. Maybe it didn't cross their minds?"

"But Mum, the house is in Dad's sole name. He could have split up with Siobhan and kicked her parents out. The fact that he never married her means that they'd be on shaky ground from a legal perspective – not to say that she wouldn't have received anything if the worst came to the worst, but it is quite a gamble, bearing in mind how controlling she is. I'd have thought she'd want the house in *her* name as it was her parents putting down most of the money? Thinking of how much money Dad would have got from the sale of the Elm Park house after half had been given to us…. I don't know. Nothing about that makes sense to me."

We both conceded defeat on this and accepted that we were never going to solve all the riddles that had arisen from hearing Harry's version of events. After I put the phone down to Mum, I called Olivia and explained to her what had happened round Harry's with the added insight from the conversation with Mum. She was a little more aloof than Mum was, and seemed like she had almost expected the fact that, according to Harry, Siobhan had acted in the way that she had. She seemed a little distant, which I put down to the fact that there was a lot to take in and maybe her natural defences had built up. After a short pause she said: "I hope you're not feeling guilty about kicking her out now. She deserves everything that she gets."

In fairness, I hadn't thought any more about that at all. I guess I had already decided to park all of that business until after Christmas and had already made my mind up that I'd get some legal advice and decide what to do, with the implications of inheritance tax and everything else at that point, but Olivia was right. I had no guilt about what happened to Siobhan anymore.

In the meantime, I had messaged Matthew, my long-lost cousin shortly after I got back from seeing Harry. I asked him when would be good to meet up for a beer. He had responded enthusiastically, saying that he'd mentioned me to his brother - my other cousin Damien, and that he was keen on meeting up too. I remembered Damien also – he was younger than Matthew and had suffered badly from asthma when he was younger. How incredible would it be to meet up with my cousins and maybe have some kind of relationship with them! If nothing else, at least some positivity had come out of this.

However, over the course of the next few days, feelings of unease grew around what Harry had told me; in particular the comment about Dad being held at knifepoint, and the delay with the death certificate persisted uncomfortably. I needed to find out more about what happened since 2004, when Dad cut ties with everyone.

My head was whirling after a long day at work and the ever growing discomfort about Dad. When I got home, I dug out Dad's death certificate to see if that provided any more clues. I read it again and it all looked very straight forward, as it had done before. Then I saw what I was looking for – the date of registration. Section 10 at the bottom. It showed 17th May 2016. Dad died on 30th April, so his death was registered around 2 and a half weeks since he died, more or less in line with Harry's account. I saw above it, just beneath the cause of death: *Certified by Mrs Caroline Beasley-Murray Senior Coroner for Essex after post-mortem without inquest.* So, there was a post-mortem examination. But why did it take so long?

After reflecting for about 15 minutes, I googled how to request a post-mortem report. I hesitated because I wasn't sure I really wanted to see what was in such a report, especially one that had been prepared for my *dad.* I'd never seen one before, and didn't know how much detail it would go into or how gruesome it would be, but in the end I just wanted to satisfy myself that everything had been dealt with properly and if it came back completely normal, then it would at least put my mind at rest a little. I wondered if he'd have scars on his body from knife wounds or maybe other signs of abuse or neglect. I shuddered at the thought of what might have happened.

It looked like every local authority had a slightly different process, but I then came across a forum. There were a surprising number of people asking how to get hold of a coroner's report and the most popular response was to write to the local coroners office and provide as much information as possible, including the reasons why you want to see it.

Although the reports are considered to be within the public domain, due to the nature of the document, they're not available online and are only provided at the discretion of the coroner. I found the Essex Coroner's Service website shortly afterwards. It provided 6 different options, although none of them included *how to ask for a post-mortem report* so I clicked on a link that said *Find or contact us.* There were options for visiting the office, a postal address, a phone number (as well as a fax number – people still use fax numbers?) and then finally an email address. I quickly drafted an email, keeping to the facts, not include any emotional language, requesting a copy of Dad's coroner's report due to concerns about his treatment prior to his death.

It was a rather frustrating two weeks that followed. Around midday the following day, Thursday 28th, I'd received a response. A response already from the Coroner's office! I wasn't expecting them to be so efficient. They were after my birth certificate showing James as my father so that they could consider my request. My stomach lurched at the thought of actually seeing the report and what it might contain. Deep breath. OK. I'd have to see if I could find it and then send them a copy.

When I got home, I rifled through boxes and files and eventually found my birth certificate, which I quickly managed to scan and send over to the Coroner's office that evening. However, then followed a number of emails backwards and forwards; the Coroner's office trying to reassure me that there was nothing that I should be concerned about, and my insistence that if that was the case then there was no reason for them to withhold the report from me.

Eventually, around mid-morning on Friday 13th December, while I was at my desk at work, the person who was dealing with me at the Coroner's office finally saw sense and sent me a scanned PDF copy of the Coroner's report. I forwarded it to my work email address and then printed it off. I didn't want to view it at my desk. My heart was beating as I collected it from the printer, and then went into a quiet meeting room at the other side of the building.

I don't know what I was expecting, but the report was only just more than one side of A4; the only thing on the second page was the signature of the Consultant Pathologist. I thought it might have been a large, bound document. I glanced up to the top of the page, which provided a summary:

I read the summary a few times. *No medication?* And he hadn't seen a GP since 2004? *Since he was first diagnosed?* She kept him prisoner for all that time with what appeared to be absolutely no medical intervention? I felt dazed at the thought. How could any coroner say that everything was in order if someone with a terminal illness, diagnosed in 2004 had no medication and was not seen by a doctor in the twelve years before they died? It was beyond madness. I couldn't understand why this had been allowed to happen. Surely there would have been follow up appointments? But then I guess he would have said he didn't want to attend? Siobhan's words coming out of his mouth yet again it would seem. I couldn't believe she was so insecure. So insecure that after getting rid of his children, isolating him from his dying mother, cutting all ties with his brother, cousin and nephew that she took it to the next extreme by preventing a doctor from seeing him after he was diagnosed with a terminal illness; I guessed this was because he might have been hospitalised and then been taken away from her. I couldn't think of the words to describe her – cruel didn't go far enough; there was an evil, selfish desperation that seemed to underpin what she'd done; none of this was how any normal, reasonable person would have behaved. She must be sociopathic or have some kind of social disorder.

For the first time I actually felt a little afraid of her and the extremes she went to. Maybe this was the reason he didn't want to marry her? But then why did he stay? Maybe she threatened him? I was suddenly reminded of the main reason I wanted to see the report – were there any scars from knife wounds shown on his body? I scanned the remainder of the document.

He had a healthy BMI of 21.3 but weighed 9st 1lb. He was only 5' 5" – much shorter than I remembered. I'd have to ask Mum how tall she remembered him to be; maybe he'd shrank due to his illness? Even so, just over 9 stone seemed incredibly light. I had visions of how thin he must have become and how his muscles would have wasted away.

Under the heading External Examination, it stated the following:

> *No scars were identified on the body. There was a small abrasion on the bridge of the nose. No significant signs of external trauma were seen.*

So, no evidence of any physical violence. I suppose the abrasion on his nose could have been his glasses rubbing? The remainder of the report sounded relatively generic; it went through each part of his body, providing the weight of major organs and commenting that each one was 'unremarkable', or that they showed no abnormality. It felt incredibly surreal to read this kind of grisly information about your father, almost made worse laid out in such a scientific and unemotional way. After studying the report for maybe a little too long I decided that I needed to get a coffee and get back to work.

"So how are you feeling now?" It had been a couple of weeks since I caught up with Jane and a lot had happened during that time. She had a child free weekend, so she had popped round to mine for dinner and I'd updated her with the latest developments.

"I feel a little exhausted," I said, and I meant it. "So much has come out over the past two months and I feel like I need a break and some time to process everything."

"I'm not surprised. Are you still thinking of talking to solicitors after Christmas?"

"Yeah. I do feel a little apprehensive about it now. I think Siobhan's the type of person who won't go down without a fight and from what I've found out, she's not likely to want to play by the rules. I was thinking of getting a Ring doorbell – you know the ones from Amazon, with a security camera?"

"Yes – that's a good idea. I guess she knows where you live! Do you think she'd come round?"

"I'm not sure – but whether there will be a row on the doorstep, or whether she'll get other people to come round to intimidate me, I'd feel safer knowing that I'd have footage of everything." I thought back to the time my mum was arrested and taken away when we were children and shuddered at the memory. What would be the lengths Siobhan would go to if she thought she was going to lose her house?

"If it makes you feel safe then it's worth it," added Jane. "She certainly sounds like a nasty lady. But at the end of the day, what due to you is due to you. If she or your dad didn't think getting a Will was worth the hassle, they've only got themselves to blame."

"I guess so. It's still such a mystery. None of this makes sense."

"Do you regret starting your search now?"

"No, I don't think so. I'm glad I've found everything out because otherwise I'd still have wondered what had happened to him and if he was still alive. None of that would have gone away, so I don't regret any of this. I just wish it was a bit of a happier story. I guess the really positive thing is that I've reconnected with my uncle and my cousin, so it's not that there's darkness without any light."

After Jane left, that question stayed with me for a little while – did I regret finding any of this out? No – it was inevitable that my curiosity would have always got the better of me; maybe it's better to know than not know; maybe if Siobhan hadn't responded to my letter, I'd still have contacted Harry; whichever way I looked at it, there was some inevitability about this.

The next few weeks were relatively uneventful compared with all the drama that had happened since September. I enjoyed to catching up with friends for Christmas drinks during lunch and after work, managed to get all my Christmas shopping done, and I had my Christmas party at work, which also doubled as my leaving do. My last day at work crept up remarkably quickly and before I knew it, there was a small group gathered round my desk staring at me and a gift bag with presents and a card was handed over. I was absolutely gobsmacked and felt pretty overwhelmed with such a send-off. I hate any kind of attention – and as a contractor, wasn't expecting any leaving gifts! I was given a bottle of gin and some gin glasses from Oliver Bonus, as well as a small box of cards – each of them suggesting different walks in London, with information on the different sights to look out for. It was incredibly thoughtful and something I was extremely grateful for. I was able to express my thanks to everyone, despite my embarrassment. They were a genuinely lovely group to work with and people that I would very much like to keep in touch with.

Christmas Day was spent at Mum's, just the two of us, and I drove us both over to see Olivia and co. on Boxing Day. It was the usual mix of good food, playing games and opening presents, and I think we all had a good time with each other. There was little discussion about Dad and what the next steps would be. Jane had given me the details of the solicitors she'd used when her husband, James, had died and I intended to get in contact with them early in the new year to initially get some advice and then decide on what to do next. I wanted to manage everyone's expectations in that I simply had no idea what more would be uncovered, and what the impact of that would be. No one could have predicted what had unravelled over the past few months and I really was prepared for anything at this stage. I reiterated that my main aim was that I didn't want to have any regrets so I wanted to tread carefully and do the right thing – but should there not be a Will or if there is room for negotiation, what's due to us should come to us.

New Year was spent with the group of friends I'd holidayed with earlier in the year. Richard and Jamie had bought a holiday cottage in Stroud the previous year and had suggested that we all come down and stay. It was brilliant fun and wonderful to get away into the countryside, enjoy long walks with good friends and properly indulge.

When I arrived back home, I ordered my Ring Doorbell, mainly as a precaution in case things became a little more animated with Siobhan, but once it was installed and linked to my phone, I felt more prepared and ready to take on the next phase of the whole Dad issue.

<u>Wednesday 8th January 2020</u>

I had telephoned Jessica Chapman at Birketts Solicitors in Chelmsford and mentioned the fact that Jane had passed her details to me. I explained the background and gave a very brief summary of what had happened so far including the fact that probate hadn't been granted and Dad's house was still in his sole name. She sounded warm and professional and we arranged an initial meeting at her office in New London Road, Chelmsford on 9th January.

The office was a converted manor house, set back off the street with a sweeping drive and landscaped gardens, and a small car park in front of the entrance. It was a beautiful building and I had slight butterflies as I walked to the door. I was relieved to have dressed relatively smartly to attend the meeting.

Jessica was as warm and as professional in person as she sounded on the phone. I had collated all the letters, documents and notes from the past few months and presented them to her. She seemed quietly impressed with my organisation and after initial introductions, coffee and biscuits arrived and she began to carefully yet swiftly read through everything. As she read Siobhan's second letter, I commented that it wasn't the nicest of letters.

"Hmmm. She's got in a couple of digs, for sure," said Jessica quietly.

"She refers to some old documents that have my full name and date of birth on them – I can't think of what she could be referring to."

"It could be anything – birth certificate, perhaps?"

"My mum kept hold of all of those documents…"

"You could always ask her?"

Presently, after she had gone through everything, including some minutes I had put together from seeing Harry and Amanda, and asking the odd question for clarity, Jessica looked up and smiled gently.

"Well, there are a few options open to you. First of all, you need to establish for sure whether Siobhan and your dad were married. And then you need to find out if there was a Will. The most straight forward way of doing that is to write to Siobhan. You have an open dialogue with her already so you could write to her yourself – or we could do that for you, but in my experience, if she receives a solicitors letter out of the blue it could start things off a little bit heavy handed, and could make things more difficult in the long run." She paused. "You were very – *nice* – in your initial letters to her and I think a more straightforward approach would work better. Just be direct; tell her exactly what you want and try not use any fluffy language. You could also ask her about the documents that she references.

"The other thing you could do in the meantime is to conduct a Certainty search. Certainty are a private company who have access to a National Will register, but will also write to all solicitors within a set radius of where your dad lived to see whether they hold a valid Will. You can google Certainty's details and do this yourself, or we could handle this for you.

"And the last thing is that while the estate is under question, you have the option of submitting a request to stop a grant of representation. This just means that it will stop anyone from settling the estate and it will last for 6 months. I can send you a link of this also if you want.

"Now – if we find that there isn't a Will, if your Dad and Siobhan were married, she has a lot more entitlement due to the rules of intestacy, but even if there *is* a Will, and assuming it leaves everything to Siobhan, we have good grounds to contest it. From the coroner's report, the fact that there was no medication administered since the year he was diagnosed with Motor Neurone Disease – and from the letter she sent to you..." she picked up Siobhan's letter and scanned through it. "Where is it... Ah – she says: '*He spent three weeks in hospital and then discharged himself when the consultant didn't arrive when he said he would, to sign for him to go home. So, he signed himself out and we got a cab and went home.*' And then she goes on to say: '*He was only willing to go back for check-ups.*'" Jessica looked up at me. "Now, despite how much in love she says she was with him, she clearly wasn't acting in his best interests. Anyone who was would have insisted that he be seen by a doctor and receive all of the care and medical assistance available to him, don't you think? They wouldn't just jump in a cab and go home, never to be seen again. And the check-ups clearly didn't happen either. If there is a Will, and it's dated around or after 2004, we could argue that your dad signed it under duress.

"The other thing to consider is whether your mum and dad ever made a Will while they were married; their divorce wouldn't revoke the Will, although, the part relating to each other become invalid. But if there's anything relating to you or your sister, this would still be legitimate, unless superseded by another Will.

"However – regardless of whether there is a Will, it's very likely that Siobhan will have some kind of claim to the house as she still lives there and I assume, would have no means of buying somewhere else. But we can cross that bridge when we get to it."

"What about the fact that she seems to have lied about my Dad still living at the address, and that she no longer does? It seems that she's masquerading as him – I guess to claim his pension and avoid paying inheritance tax? What's your view on all of that?"

"I can really comment on that. All I can advise you about at the moment is the next steps to take if there is or isn't a Will."

I drove home in deep thought about the next steps. It had been a beautifully crisp January day and the sun was low in the crimson sky, maybe about half an hour before it set. I felt a little deflated at the thought that Jessica was unwilling to grab hold of how much Siobhan had lied. It felt like a missed opportunity, but this was the initial meeting and maybe more advice along that route would be forthcoming the further down the road we went. The next steps did sound interesting and I had a little more investigation to do before I formally engaged Birketts. Thinking back how asking whether Dad and Siobhan were married appeared to have caused her bitterness to erupt, I felt reluctant to ask Siobhan this question again. But maybe there was another option available.

<u>**Thursday 9th January 2020**</u>

As I walked towards the Essex Records Office the following morning, I marvelled at how much had I'd discovered since I was last here. I had decided not to tell Mum or Olivia about my meeting with Jessica just yet. I needed to get my head straight first. I knew they'd both be chomping at the bit to evict Siobhan and sell the house, but thinking of how determined and brutal she appeared and how difficult the potential court case would be, not even taking into account how much this would all cost in legal fees, (without any guarantee of any outcome in our favour,) I wanted to be clear in my own head before I said anything to them.

Before I knew it, I had climbed the glass staircase and was at the all too familiar receptionist's window. A different, older lady was on duty today and the office behind her was buzzing with activity. She smiled as I approached her.

"Hello there, can I help you?"

"Hi, yes, I hope so. I need to see if I can get a marriage certificate, if possible."

"I'll buzz you in."

The door to the left buzzed and I walked through, surprised that this time no passes were required. I stood at the counter on the other side and the receptionist swivelled round in her chair to greet me.

"So... Do you have the names of the people in question?"

"Yes – here they are." I pushed a piece of paper towards her with Dad's and Siobhan's names on it. I had also included Dad's date of birth.

"Right.... And do you have the date they were married?"

"Erm, no. I, err, I don't actually know if they *were* married. Is there any way of finding out?"

The receptionist screwed up her face but remained friendly. "Let me see what I can uncover," she said with a gentle smile. She turned and walked behind what looked like a large filing cabinet, with a couple of pcs inside, as well as floor to ceiling paper files. I waited, watching the other people milling around behind where I stood. It had a relaxed, friendly atmosphere. Within about 10 minutes, the receptionist emerged from behind the filing cabinet and looked at me quizzically.

"Do you have a copy of James's death certificate?"

"Yes – I have it here." I pulled it out of my pocket, unfolded it and passed it across to her.

"Now – you see. The answer was here all along. They were not married." She pointed to the mid-section of the death certificate, where it showed the Informant's Qualification as *'causing the body to be cremated'*. "You see that Siobhan is the informant? If she *was* married to James, it would show the qualification as 'spouse' or 'wife'; the fact that is says *'causing the body to be cremated'* is just a default option. If anyone not related to James – a council worker or a neighbour, for example, would have been the informant, it would have had something like that as the qualification."

There was something darkly satisfying about Siobhan being classified as the equivalent of a council worker in the context of Dad's death certificate. I was a little surprised that Jessica hadn't thought to look at this detail; I guess this is a pretty unique situation and most other cases she's dealt with were maybe more straightforward? Last night I had already applied to Certainty for a Will search, at a cost of £140, and had placed a hold on anyone attempting to settle Dad's estate, which cost a further £20. The timescale for Certainty to finalise their search and provide feedback was 28 days, so I'd added a reminder in my calendar to follow up with them if required. When I got home, I quickly typed out a letter to Siobhan. Taking Jessica's advice, I kept it short, sharp and to the point. I also wanted to know what documents she had, which had my personal information on them:

Dear Siobhan

Many thanks for your letter.

You mentioned that you have some old documents with my full name and date of birth on them. Can you advise what these documents are? (I know they don't include my birth certificate as my dad didn't take it when he left.)

In addition, I have since discovered that a grant of probate has not yet been issued so it would be helpful to know if my dad left a Will. If so, please can I have a copy.

Many thanks and best wishes,

Colin

I posted the letter that afternoon, feeling more determined that things were now beginning to happen and maybe some more answers would arrive soon. However, I was also relieved that I'd invested in my Ring doorbell.

It was another nice bright afternoon, and I had a leisurely walk home from the post-box, stopping off for a take-out latte at Coffee Squared. I did feel relatively relaxed and tended to enjoy the period immediately after a contract finished. It gave me some time to reflect and catch up with myself. I had thought about maybe going to Iceland to see the Northern Lights, but had decided against it with all the Dad and Siobhan stuff that would be going on; I'd rather concentrate on that rather than go away and worry about not be able to respond to emails. Maybe it would wait for another year. I did need to think about getting another job though – I'd spoken to a few agencies and there were a couple of opportunities but nothing concrete just yet.

I got in and called Mum to provide an update.

"Hi Mum, it's me."

"Hi Dear, how have you been?"

"I'm good thanks – are you ok?"

"Yes, yes, all good."

"I thought I'd let you know the latest with Dad and Siobhan. I went to see a solicitor yesterday to get some initial advice." Mum fell silent, listening intently. "It was quite useful – I gave her all the letters and documents that I'd collated over the past few months and she went through everything..."

"Did you... did you tell her that she said my marriage was a sham?"

I rolled my eyes and gave out a large sigh. "Mum. Honestly, *you have to let this go.* She read everything and took everything into account. She's a solicitor. She would have seen much worse things than that! After everything else Siobhan has done, that really is the least of it!"

"But my marriage was also about the two of you – was she also saying that you were a sham? He *loved* you. I know he did, and I don't know what snapped in him to change his mind. Well, other than *her*." Mum spoke with understated passion and emotion, pent up from years long passed. She did have a habit of putting herself at the centre of everything and focussing on the smallest issues that meant the most to her without really thinking about the bigger picture. At the same time, I was all too aware that a solicitor would look more at the legal side than the emotional implications of a few choice words to an ex-wife.

The conversation between me and Mum continued. She confirmed that while they were still married, She and Dad had never got round to thinking about Wills so there was no chance of anything being left to me and Olivia on the basis of that. I then told her what had transpired – the follow up letter to Siobhan, as well as the hold on the estate and the Certainty Will search, to which she listened to with interest, although I could tell she was still clinging on to the point that Siobhan had wronged her. To change the subject onto happier things, I then suggested contacting Harry again and seeing if we could arrange a date to go round and see him and Amanda as a group.

"OK, well maybe in the spring, once the weather warms up a bit." Mum, having a bit of a travel phobia never liked travelling, especially in the dark, so this sounded like a good idea.

I called Olivia straight after and talked her through what had happened and the letter I'd sent to Siobhan.

"I can't wait until we can evict her!" She sounded a little tense.

"I think you have to bear in mind that there's no guarantee of us winning or coming out of this with anything. What I've learned from this is to expect the unexpected, so don't be disappointed if we fall at the first hurdle."

"OK – well it'll be interesting to see what happens next."

"I think we have to be prepared for whatever happens. If it goes to court it could get pretty nasty, not to think of the cost."

"Like I said before, you don't have to do this on your own - I'll support you in court." I wondered how much of this was bravado and when it came down to it, if Olivia would want to, or be able to cope with the court hearing. It obviously wouldn't be an enjoyable experience – but seeing Siobhan again after all these years, after everything we'd learned would be terribly difficult. I decided to steer the conversation away onto other things.

"How are things, generally? Are you OK?"

Olivia sighed as she complained of another row with Kirstie, (in my opinion blown all out of proportion) but I let her vent for a few minutes before the call finished.

<u>**Thursday 23rd January 2020**</u>

The next few days I got on with some jobs around the house –
I painted my hallway and tidied a few cupboards – nice
mundane jobs to while away miserable January days.

I also had an interview for a new job. It was for an
Operations Manager for a Marine and Offshore Energy insurer
and it seemed to go pretty well. The ladies that interviewed
me were friendly and encouraging and I think I got everything
across that I needed to. Although I quite enjoyed the quieter
pace of life when I was in between jobs (and I had enough
money from contracting to tide me by for a while), it would
still be nice to get back into the routine of work again. Fingers
crossed it would go to the next stage. It was also an
opportunity to meet up with former colleagues for lunch and
catch up on the office gossip. It made me realise how much I
missed the city and felt a little spark of adrenaline at the
thought of starting something new and getting back in the
swing of things.

As I travelled back from Liverpool Street, I glanced out
of the window as I passed the Olympic Park at Stratford. It
made me think immediately of Harry and Amanda, who lived
a couple of minutes away – and then I realised I hadn't heard
back from Matthew about meeting up for a beer with him and
Damien. I quickly typed a text to him, and was surprised when
I received a response within a few minutes:

```
    Hi Matthew, belated happy new year!  Hope
    all good with you.  It would be great to
    catch up if you're still up for a beer.
                    Let me know when suits.


OK Colin, I'll let you know mate.  Happy
new year to you.  This year has started
very busy - it's a good thing, not
```

I felt a little disappointed at Matthew's response. Maybe he was very busy at the moment; being self- employed he might be completely run off his feet. But the more I thought about it, the more I wondered if he'd reconsidered wanting to meet up. Was he reluctant to see me, thinking I'd just rake through the past? I wonder if he'd spoken to Harry and he'd put him off? I walked home trying not to feel paranoid.

At the weekend, Jane and I travelled into London to see the musical Hamilton. It was her Christmas present to me and it was amazing! It was also good to see Jane and talk things through with her. I'd explained that I hadn't yet had a response from Siobhan and was mulling over when I should chase her up. Jane suggested giving it another week which I thought was fair.

<u>**Friday 31st January 2020**</u>

As nothing had been forthcoming from Siobhan and it had been three weeks since my last letter to her, I decided to chase her up by recorded delivery. Ultimately, I wanted to progress things as quickly as possible, so I thought about Jessica's advice again and drafted a very to-the-point letter:

Dear Siobhan

Conscious that I haven't had a response to my previous letter dated 9th January, attached.

The absence of a reply suggests that my dad did not leave a Will when he died. On this basis and as next of kin, I intend to make an application for the grant of probate in my name and instruct solicitors to commence proceedings. If you are aware of any reason why I should not do this, please let me know within 7 days from the date of this letter.

If I don't hear from you within 7 days, I shall assume that you're happy for me to take this action.

Many thanks and best wishes

Colin

I felt resolute as I paid for the postage and received the receipt for the recorded delivery. I hadn't the need for sending anything recorded delivery for many years, and was pleased to see you could track the delivery of the item online, so I'd be able to see exactly when Siobhan received my letter!

I logged on the following day and saw that an attempt had been made to delivery my letter, but there was no one in to sign for it, so it had been taken back to the sorting office. Of course she wouldn't answer the door, but I wondered whether the postman saw the curtains twitching this time. I checked the Royal Mail website over next couple of days to see if Siobhan had collected my letter – but it wasn't until 3rd February that it was updated to show that she had finally collected it. What would her next move be?

<u>**Wednesday 5th February 2020**</u>

I was woken up by a knock at the door. I pulled some jeans on and tried to make myself look half presentable as I rushed down the stairs. It was the postlady, who handled me a letter and asked me to sign for it – it was Recorded and Guaranteed Next Day Delivery. I couldn't wait to hear what Siobhan had to say for herself. I marvelled at the envelope as I closed the door – I could see she'd paid £6.60 for postage alone.

Dear Colin

Regarding your letter, the Court document that I mentioned, containing your name and d.o.b. was the Bow County Court Decree Nisi document dated 19th Feb 1985 – No. of Matter 85-D-1011. I'm sure that if you need to see the Decree Nisi your mother would have had the identical document.

As far as wanting a copy of James's Will, my solicitor has informed me that because neither any of your family, nor any of James's family are named as either executor nor beneficiary, then I am not required to hand over a copy of the Will.

I hope that explains things clearly.

Yours

Siobhan

I don't know what I expected, but I could feel my blood pressure rising as I read Siobhan's letter. I reread her original letter and nowhere did it refer to any court papers – just that she'd dug out some *'old documents'*, so I felt justified in asking for clarity on that issue, which did now make sense. The other point that I allowed to get to me, maybe a little too much, was how she differentiated between *my family* and *James's family*, as if we weren't even related. Regardless of what had happened in the past, and who she blamed, he was, and will have always been my dad. As I reread her previous letter, nowhere did she refer to him as 'your dad', just James. In contrast, Harry's letter, as well as being much warmer in tone, always referred to him as 'your dad'.

I lingered on the point about her solicitor advising her that she didn't need to hand over a copy of Dad's Will and wondered why a solicitor would provide such advice. Maybe there was a Will; maybe there wasn't. If she sent me a copy of it and it showed that neither me nor Olivia were beneficiaries, then, depending on the date of the Will, I guess that would be the end of it. The Recorded Guaranteed Next Day Delivery seemed like a lot of effort to just tell me to go away. There must be more to it.

I called Jessica at Birketts and explained what had happened since we last met. It felt that now would be the right time to formally engage solicitors for them to take it to the next level. I arranged to meet her again and go over the options available.

I had to sign a number of forms to formally engage them, and this time, Jessica arranged for letters and notes to be photocopied so she had copies for her file. The outcome we agreed would be that she would write to Siobhan asking for a copy of Dad's Will. She suggested mentioning that if she refuses, we could make an application with the court, requiring her to produce a copy of the Will by law – she said that in her experience it had never come to this; the threat of court action was usually enough to produce a result.

Once we have a copy of the Will, we might be able to challenge it on a number of grounds – mainly whether any undue influence was used, but Jessica said she'd provide further advice if any points became relevant. If there was no Will, me and my sister would be entitled to make an application for grant of probate, but Siobhan would very likely have a strong claim and she'd have 6 months from the date of the grant to do so. I could envision this becoming a very long drawn out and painful experience.

Jessica said that she'd draft a letter to Siobhan and send it to me for approval within the coming days.

<u>Tuesday 18th February 2020</u>

During the week, I started my new job, the one I'd had my initial interview for. I'd had a second interview a couple of weeks later and then agreed a quick start date, which I was happy with. My first day went well – the team reporting into me seemed like a nice group of people with a good mix of experience, and first impressions were positive. There looked like there was a lot of opportunity to make improvements and implement new things, so I was keen to get stuck in.

I also received the draft letter from Jessica, which was everything I expected it to be: Professional, well written and formal enough to scare Siobhan into thinking we meant business. It gave her a 14 day deadline to respond, which I thought was fair. I sent a quick response to Jessica to confirm the letter was fine and I was happy for her to send it. She confirmed back that it would be sent by Recorded Delivery that day. I wondered how long it would take for Siobhan to collect this one from the sorting office.

I spoke to my Mum over the weekend to let her know how my first week in the new job had gone and update her on the latest with Siobhan. I also raised the point about going to see Harry again. The nights were finally getting lighter and spring was definitely in the air. Mum hesitated before saying that she didn't think it was the best idea to see him now.

"Why not? You were so keen last year when I went round on my own." I was gobsmacked by this U-turn.

"Well, you said that he was a bit overwhelmed and I'm not sure he really wants us to go round and bother him again."

"What do you mean? We were *invited* round! Amanda wants to cook us all lunch!"

"No, I don't think so."

"But think about Olivia and Louise – Olivia specifically asked me to arrange it with Harry so that Louise can meet her extended family!"

"I'm not sure Olivia really wants to go round now."

"*What?* Why not?"

"Like I said, we just think that he'll be a bit overwhelmed by us all turning up at once."

"Where are you getting this information from? Nothing has changed since I saw him last!"

"I don't want him to feel we're pressuring him into it."

I was incredibly frustrated at mum's refusal to listen to me and to disregard anything I said to reassure her than Harry and Amanda had invited us round. Something had clearly been discussed between Mum and Olivia I had no idea why things had changed so much – last year Mum was begging me to take her round to see them both, but it was me who had to put the brakes on. I thought back to the conversation I'd had with Olivia straight after I'd seen Harry and even then she seemed a little lukewarm. I needed to understand what was behind this. I called her shortly after I put the phone down to Mum and after a little small talk, I asked her when she wanted to see Harry.

"Oh, why are you bringing this up again? Mum said she'd speak to you about it."

"Why didn't *you* speak to me about it?" I could feel myself getting a bit hot. "Olivia – I don't understand – you really wanted me to say to Harry that Louise wanted to meet some of her relatives and get to know her extended family. What's changed?"

"Why do you want us to be one big happy family? It's not going to happen!"

"Where is this coming from? I never said we'd be one big happy family! I just think that Harry is the *only* family we have now, other than mum and each other, and why wouldn't we want to reconnect with him? I'm not saying we see him every week, but maybe once or twice a year! And it was you who specifically asked to see him!"

"But Harry doesn't want to see us, does he? You said yourself that he was overwhelmed…"

"That was when I spoke to him on the phone! He and Amanda were so welcoming when I went round there – and we were *all* invited for lunch. You've put me in a really difficult position, Liv."

"But you said that Matthew was going to meet up with you and he doesn't want to now, does he?"

"Look, I don't know – he said he was busy with work and he's self-employed – but I'm talking about Harry, not Matthew."

Olivia paused. "I'll still come to court with you and support you if it comes to that."

"You'd rather come to court and face the woman who took our dad away than to have lunch with our uncle who wants to see us?"

"I just don't feel comfortable. I'd rather just leave it. I don't want to stir everything up again!"

I came off the phone frustrated that Olivia had managed to convince Mum not to go to see Harry, just because she'd changed her mind. I wasn't really sure how to explain how they'd shifted their position about everything and thought it would look a little odd for me to turn up on my own again after the conversation last time about how keen everyone was to reconnect. It would have been better for her to have said upfront that she didn't want to see Harry and then I could have managed it in a better way with them. And to think I'd made contact with Harry myself – on my own – taken the risk of being rejected and opened the door to reconnect with our family again. Maybe Olivia needed some time to get her head round it, but it surprised me how eager she was to have her day in court, which would be so much harder mentally and emotionally. Maybe it was because Harry wasn't going to give us a share of his house that she wasn't interested.

My phone buzzed while I was at my desk. It was an email from Jessica:

> Hi Colin
> I hope you're well.
> I have today received the attached letter from Siobhan. I have not yet received a copy of the Will from her solicitor but will see if this has materialised by the end of the 14 day deadline we gave, and if not we can decide what action to take at that point.
> Kind regards
> Jessica

Jessica had attached a scanned copy of Siobhan's letter. I tapped on the PDF attachment and read Siobhan's letter with interest:

> *Dear Ms Chapman*
>
> *Re your letter of 18th Feb 2020, as requested I have asked my solicitors (Hook and Partners) to write to you and provide you with a copy of my late partner's Will.*
>
> *I feel that if I sent you a copy, your client would most probably not believe that it was genuine. I can guarantee that a copy will be sent to your offices as soon as possible.*
>
> *I had already written to your client on 4th Feb and informed him that neither he nor his*

I glowered at my phone. The part where she suggested I wouldn't be willing to believe her! If she'd just sent me a copy of the Will, then solicitors wouldn't have had to get involved and this would have been more straight forward. I wondered what would materialise, if anything. From her behaviour, she must be trying to hide something. But then I thought back to the first email I'd had from Harry when he said that Siobhan kept her cards very close to her chest. I again felt irritation at how she implied I had no connection to my dad.

I called Jessica and had a brief chat with her during my lunch break. I remembered that I hadn't heard back from Certainty about the Will search and I asked her whether it would be appropriate to let them know that the Will was allegedly at Hook and Partners. Jessica agreed and suggested I chase them up on progress.

I quickly sent Certainty an email alerting them of the lead we'd received and asked them for a progress update.

<u>Friday 28th February 2020</u>

My phone buzzed indicating an email had arrived – something else from Jessica. Surely this wasn't Siobhan's solicitor getting in touch with us already?

> Hi Colin
> I have now received the attached letter and copy Will from Siobhan (rather from her solicitor). A copy from a solicitor confirming they hold the original would be better because if the original Will cannot be located, and it was known to be in the deceased's own possession then there is a (rebuttable) presumption that the Will was revoked by destruction.
> On the face of it, the Will appears to be validly executed. This does not, of course, explain why a Grant of Probate has not been extracted nor why the property title has not been dealt with.
> Please do let me know what you would like to do next. Did the Certainty Will search find anything – a later Will perhaps?
> Kind regards
> Jessica

I looked at both attachments and opened Siobhan's letter first:

> *After speaking to my solicitors again, they inform me that it would be much quicker if I sent you a copy of my late partner's Will.*
>
> *Please find enclosed.*

And with a deep breath, I opened the Will attachment. It had been drafted by Meadows and Moran in Romford, a different solicitors to Hook and Partners, who Siobhan had previously mentioned.

> *THIS IS THE LAST WILL AND TESTAMENT of me JAMES EDWARD WALTERS of 181A Danesdale Road South Hackney London E9 5RN*
>
> 1. *I HEREBY REVOKE all former Wills and Testamentary dispositions made by me and declare this only to contain my last Will and Testament*
> 2. *I GIVE DEVISE AND BEQUEATH all my real and personal property whatsoever and wheresoever situate not hereby or by any codicil hereto otherwise specifically disposed of SUBJECT to the payment of my debts funeral and testamentary expenses unto SIOBHAN PATRICIA O'REILLY if and only if she survives me by twenty eight days absolutely and appoint her to be the sole executrix hereof*
> 3. *I DESIRE to be buried*
>   *IN WITNESS whereof I have hereunto set my hand to this 10 day of July 1995*

So, it was true – everything was left to her. *But he wanted to be buried, not cremated.* Why would she cremate him and not bury him? Could this be proof of another, later Will? As I read it again, I noticed the date of the Will. Not only would this be nearly a decade before he was diagnosed with Motor Neurone Disease, it was also 2 days after Olivia's 21st birthday. I remembered vividly the celebrations we had for her 21st. Her birthday was on the Saturday and she was dating a guy who lived in Croydon, so a small group of us went there for the weekend, ended up in a nasty club that was playing some really bad industrial dance music, and then after far too many drinks, tried to get into the local park by scaling the locked gates. I remember how hilarious this was because Olivia got stuck halfway up and had to be rescued by her boyfriend. You kind of had to be there at the time!

But while this was going on, Dad was planning to leave everything in his Will to Siobhan. He must have remembered Olivia's birthday and that it was her 21st. I couldn't help wonder if there was some significance to this, rather than it being a coincidence. Remembering that they moved into the house in Canvey early 1996, maybe it was around this time that they were getting all their affairs in order, in preparation for the move? I again thought it was strange that despite the Will, the house remained in his sole name and they were never married.

During my lunch break I called Jessica to talk it through with her. She reiterated that the Will did appear to be legitimate, but she would have preferred an official copy from Siobhan's solicitors; she also said that it was very short and uncomplicated with no room for any interpretation, so there was no reason it wasn't sent to us in the first place. Jessica also didn't believe the reason that Siobhan sent it herself to save time. Jessica received similar requests frequently and can easily turn them around within 24 hours; it was also received before the 3rd March deadline, so not as though time had run out.

I asked about whether it was likely that another Will had superseded this one due to the fact that it stated that Dad wanted to be buried and he ended up being cremated. Jessica agreed that this was possible, however, burial wishes are not legally binding, because someone might change their mind on their death bed and a subsequent conversation could have taken place without it being documented. I considered this, but the more I thought about it, the more I came to the conclusion that Siobhan, again just wanted him all to herself. As well as cutting off his family, isolating him from doctors, she decided to cremate him so she could keep him in a jar on the mantel, away from anyone else.

Jessica suggested I write to Siobhan again, asking why the estate had not been settled nearly 4 years after his death. By law, you have 6 months to settle the estate, or least start proceedings, so she expressed some confusion at the legal advice Siobhan had received; my view was that it was due to inheritance tax. Siobhan wasn't married to Dad. She had never worked so would not be eligible for any kind of state pension and if she settled the estate based on the Will, she'd have to sell the house in order to pay for the substantial inheritance tax bill as there would be no spousal exclusion. So, in order to keep everything she had, she chose to masquerade as Dad. I shook my head as I thought of how my letters to her and all the things I'd subsequently found out had threatened everything she owned and was desperately clinging on to. No wonder she was so bitter. If only she'd handled it differently; if she'd written back to me within a week, using kinder language and a warmer tone then I probably wouldn't have felt the need to take the route that I did. Despite Jessica's suggestion, I decided not to write to Siobhan again – I could imagine the response I'd get back - although it would be interesting to see what the Certainty Search would uncover.

I called Certainty to find out the outcome of their search. I spoke to a lady called Sally, who was friendly and very helpful. She was able to confirm that Hook and Partners had been included in the original search, but had not responded to the request, which was not unusual; solicitors would only respond if they had a Will that matched the search. However, when they received my email, she contacted them again and had spoken to the Partner, who confirmed that they did not hold a Will for Dad. Why would Siobhan try to assure us that Hook and Partners held the Will when this wasn't the case, only to provide a copy of an apparently genuine Will within days? I guessed that she hadn't even engaged a solicitor and was acting off her own volition. Maybe she felt the need to include how she had engaged solicitors to add gravitas to her position? I asked whether Meadows and Moran (the solicitors who'd drafted Dad's Will) were included within the search and Sally advised that as they were based in Romford, they were outside of the catchment area for where Dad lived, so they were not included.

Shortly afterwards I called Meadows and Moran, who were able to confirm they did hold a copy of Dad's Will, but were unable to confirm any details as I was not named as Executor or Beneficiary. After I told them I had a copy of a Will from 1995, the lady I spoke to said this was the latest Will they were aware of, but wouldn't know if a different Will had superseded it if it was held at a different firm.

With a sigh, I came to the final conclusion that this was it. We'd come to the end of the line and my search was over.

I called Jessica again to update her on what I'd found out. I was also curious to know what would happen when Siobhan died. As Dad's house is still in his sole name and

Siobhan presumably had no intention of settling the estate, would intestacy rules still apply without her around? It unfortunately wasn't as straight forward as that. When Siobhan dies, Dad's Will is still valid, so her executors would have to work through Dad's estate first, and then if Siobhan has a Will, they'd ensure her estate is then settled according to her wishes. If she doesn't have a Will, the house will become property of the state.

I travelled home on the train, reflecting on what the last few weeks had uncovered. I felt a mixture of emotions – sadness, uneasiness, and admittedly a little bit of relief that I guess this saga had come to an end. So many thoughts swirled around my head. I thought about the life that Dad could have had and all the missed opportunities. I reflected on Mum and Olivia not wanting to see Harry again and wondered how I could get around that. But a small spark of anger steadily grew the more I thought about Siobhan and how her deception, manipulation and bitter insecurity had led to Dad losing everything. Me and Olivia lost our dad. My nan lost her son. Harry lost his brother. *And Siobhan got everything.* It just seemed so terribly unfair and as I walked from the station, the anger at the injustice of it all grew and grew.

When I got home, I was Incandescent with rage. I needed to do something about this, but I didn't know what to do. Then I opened my laptop and googled "Inheritance Tax Fraud", which took me to a government website about how to report tax evasion. Within a few minutes, I'd filled in an online form with Siobhan's details and her address and the reasons why I thought tax evasion had occurred. I typed furiously and without any hesitation, knowing that she would know immediately who would have betrayed her. I wanted her to know. I wanted her to know that it was me who alerted the authorities to what a conniving deceitful bitch she was. I

wanted to her to know that she was about to lose her house –
sorry – *Dad's house* – because of me. I wanted her to know
that what goes around fucking comes around and if she'd been
even the slightest bit kinder none of this would have
happened. I wanted to teach her the biggest lesson of her
small, sorry, miserable life.

I was just about to click the submit button, sending all
this information to a fraud officer who'd probably jump at the
chance to pay Siobhan a visit and possibly even arrest her. I
could picture the curtains twitching as they threatened to kick
in the door to gain entry. But then something stopped me. I
have no idea why I didn't click the button, but I suddenly
remembered my words to Olivia – *'I didn't want to do anything
that I later regretted.'* Would I have regrets about this? What
would I gain from doing this? Would Dad be cheering
encouragement or screaming at me to stop? *Was it actually
my civic duty to do this?* Do I really want to sink to her level?

Anger gave in to confusion and sorrow, and I cleared
the form and closed my laptop.

<u>Sunday 14th March 2021</u>

Over a year has passed since the drama of Dad's Will. Shortly after I considered reporting Siobhan to HMRC, we were plunged into a nationwide lockdown due to the Coronavirus outbreak. It came as a shock to most people, mainly because of the government's laisse faire attitude initially, which made everyone think it was just a severe type of flu. Over 100,000 people in the UK have since died, with millions more around the world, and we're now in the third national lockdown. At least there is a vaccine, which is being rolled out at pace so hope that a return to normal life by some point this year is keeping everyone going.

I found the lockdown incredibly difficult, especially at first. Over-night everything changed – from my busy, varied life, commuting into the city, meeting friends and colleagues for lunch and drinks after work, and packed, exciting weekends – to literally nothing; working from home and spending all my time alone. My highlight was my weekly trip to Sainsbury's on a Friday evening. I had phone calls and video calls with friends, but it wasn't the same as seeing people in the flesh, going out for a meal, going to the cinema; getting away for the weekend; *living a life*. I found I had a lot of time to reflect on what happened with Dad, and to try to come to terms with not just the past 6 months, but the impact my dad had on my life since he left us. From all the thoughts invading my head, I came up with the idea of writing everything down; getting it all out of my head so I wasn't constantly thinking about all the ifs, buts and maybes. I'm happy that I don't regret anything I did, which ended up being my main objective in the end. But I also don't regret *not* doing anything – mainly I don't regret not reporting Siobhan to HMRC. Admittedly, it's still something that crosses my mind from time to time, but I think doing so would just shake everything up again unnecessarily and I'd prefer not to create any more drama, at least at the moment.

When I started out, my first goal was to achieve closure; so, did I get close to achieving my goal? Maybe in some ways. It stopped the wondering and the nagging questions that had persisted since I was a child, but inevitably uncovered some other uncomfortable truths. Dad's love for Siobhan, or his fear of her, or his need to be controlled by her – maybe a combination of all of the above – overshadowed anything else in his life, including me, my sister, his brother and his mum. I don't think I'll ever understand that, but I have to keep reminding myself that it wasn't personal to me, despite how much it felt personal at the time. In fact, it still feels personal if I think about it too much, especially if I think about Dad's relationship with Steve. Having said that, I do now wonder whether his closeness to Steve was born out of regret over his decision to cut ties with us.

I still don't understand why Dad and Siobhan never decided to marry, and why the house was left in his sole name, despite the Will. Siobhan's initial letter seemed warm, albeit cautious, but she appeared to take offence at the question of whether they got married or had children, which makes me think there is another story to tell that could explain this, but I don't think we'll ever get to the bottom of that. I sometimes think about Harry's revelation about Dad allegedly being threatened at knife point and the more I've considered it, the less credible this claim seems. I spoke to a friend on Zoom about it and they suggested that Dad could have got involved with some gangster who threatened him and his family, and he cut ties with us to protect us all – but I can't see how this could be true, and if it was, I'm sure there would have been other hints or clues that would have supported this theory. I wonder if Dad, knowing that he had no viable explanation for cutting ties with us, but also knowing that questions were being asked, came out with something that Harry (and whomever else challenged him) were not able to question, and so he kept to that story; he may have even come to believe it himself at some level. I have often wondered whether he was happy or whether he felt pressured into doing what he did; especially at the times when he was incapacitated and completely cut off from the world, with only Siobhan for company. Maybe he got everything he wanted? I have to come to terms with the fact that this is something I'll never know.

I have exchanged a couple of emails with Harry. Each time I emailed him, he has come back quickly the same day with a warm, enthusiastic response. Lockdown has been the best excuse to postpone the planned visit and I've since talked over the possibility of going to see Harry with my mum a few times, who has now been convinced that yes, Harry does want to see us and would welcome us for lunch when it's safe to do so. I haven't discussed it with Olivia because I'd rather not create any further issues with her. I've thought this through, and I guess that despite her initial enthusiasm to meet Harry and introduce Louise to him, I understand that after a period of reflection she may have got cold feet, fearing the opening up old wounds and ghosts from the past, none of which she's ready to face just yet. Maybe after Mum and I go to see Harry, and she hears what a wonderful time we had with him and Amanda, she might come round to the idea. But I will leave it up to her to make that decision.

I never heard back from my cousin Matthew. Maybe I will get to meet up for a beer with him and Damien when lockdown ends, and life returns to normal. It would be great to hear his side of the story, but it would also be amazing to reconnect with another member of my family who I'd never thought I'd get to see again.

In the summer, I finally summoned enough courage to make an enquiry about getting some counselling. I now see my counsellor every Thursday evening at 8pm and talk through some of the issues on my mind. Inevitably, Dad was a common topic of conversation during the earlier sessions. It was sometimes quite emotional to talk about what had happened and to be asked questions about how I felt - things I'd never really thought about in the way I was being asked - in such detail. Although we've moved on to other issues, Dad is inevitably linked to many of my barriers, insecurities and confidence issues, as well as shame, guilt and suppressed anger (but then so are a number of other things). Sometimes we go into complete unchartered territory and sometimes there are a few 'aha!' moments which really help me understand the feelings I have and what I should do to feel better and live a more fulfilled life. Sometimes just understanding the root causes of why I feel a certain way helps lessen the power of those feelings. I often wonder if things would have been different if Dad had received counselling, to talk through some of the issues he had around his need to be controlled, which resulted in cutting ties with everyone. From the benefit I've had in understanding myself more, I have often wondered what the root causes of his feelings and subsequent actions were.

My initial expectation of counselling was that it would help me overcome all my insecurities and fears and I'd emerge as a perfect version of me, whatever that means. I now realise that counselling won't fix me, but it will help me in understanding myself and accepting my imperfections, or what I consider to be imperfections. This in itself is empowering, but it's a long journey that I've only just begun. I think it also starts with trying to be the best person I can be and helping the people I love as much as I can. But also, being kinder to myself. Currently a work in progress.